SENEGAL

SENEGAL

An African Nation Between Islam and the West

Sheldon Gellar

Westview Press • Boulder, Colorado

Gower • Hampshire, England

Profiles / Nations of Contemporary Africa

Copyright © 1982 by Westview Press, Inc.

Published in 1982 in the United States of America by
  Westview Press, Inc.
  5500 Central Avenue
  Boulder, Colorado 80301
  Frederick A. Praeger, President and Publisher

Published in 1982 in Great Britain by
  Gower Publishing Company Limited
  Gower House, Croft Road
  Aldershot, Hampshire GU11 3HR, England

Library of Congress Cataloging in Publication Data
Gellar, Sheldon.
  Senegal – an African nation between Islam and the West.
  (Profiles. Nations of contemporary Africa)
  Bibliography: p.
  Includes index.
  1. Senegal. I. Title. II. Series.
DT549.22.G44   1982   966'.3   82-15946
ISBN 0-89158-837-X

British Library Cataloguing in Publication Data
Gellar, Sheldon
  Senegal. – (Profiles, nations of contemporary Africa)
  1. Senegal
  I. Title   II. Series
  966'.3   DT549.5
  ISBN 0-566-00551-4

Printed and bound in the United States of America

To my parents,
Jerry and Sally Gellar

Contents

Figures and Tables

Tables

Preface

I met Ismaila Dia, my Senegalese "big brother," in 1962 on board the French liner *Ancerville* sailing from Marseilles to Dakar. Ismaila was returning to Senegal after nearly a decade of studies in France, where he had obtained advanced degrees in biology and pharmacology, while I was on my way to Senegal to do fieldwork for my doctoral dissertation.

Ismaila wore impeccably tailored French woollen suits and read *Le Monde* and the French Communist daily, *L'Humanité*, regularly. Despite outward appearances, Ismaila was no Black Frenchman. He came from a noble Tukolor family on the Senegal River. His father, who died when Ismaila was a young boy, had been a respected Muslim religious leader. Ismaila himself went to Koranic schools in Mauritania before attending and excelling in French colonial public schools in Saint Louis.

Over the years, as the memories of French colonial rule receded more and more into the past, Ismaila, like Senegal, became both more cosmopolitan and more traditional. Although he still read French newspapers and magazines, France was no longer the only focal point of Western culture for him. He sent a younger brother to Germany to study engineering. Like many of his countrymen, he developed an interest in learning English. At the same time, Islam became a more important part of his life. He went on pilgrimage to Mecca. He came to prefer the traditional African *boubou* to Western clothes.

Ismaila Dia took me under his protection and brought me into the family circle. Through him and his family, I was able to develop more than just an academic interest in Senegal. We shared personal and family triumphs and tragedies. In my periodic trips to Senegal during the past twenty years, I watched Ismaila and Senegal change as the country gradually shed the weight of its colonial past and asserted its own national identity. Without renouncing its strong ties to France and the West, Senegal has moved closer to the Islamic world and played an increasingly active role in international politics. Despite its small population (6 million) and limited natural resources, Senegal has become one of the most influential nations in Black Africa.

In 1962, Dakar had but one traffic light and the great mosque of Touba had not yet been completed. The legacy of French colonial rule was very evident. French officials still occupied most of the upper echelons of the Senegalese civil service; Renaults, Peugeots, and Citroëns monopolized traffic; and the peanut dominated the economic life of the country.

Twenty years later, Dakar is no longer an excolonial capital but a modern cosmopolitan city with daily traffic jams and embassies representing more than fifty nations. The Senegalese bureaucracy has been Africanized, and French cars must now share the roads with Hondas, Volkswagens, and Mercedes. Islam no longer merely coexists with French culture; it has become ascendant.

In the countryside, the peasantry is less docile and more demanding of the government. Political life has revived as Senegal's ruling party and eleven opposition parties prepare for the 1983 national elections in one of Black Africa's rare multiparty democracies. Change is in the air. And Senegalese look to a more hopeful future despite the nation's current economic woes.

This book provides the reader with a general introduction to Senegal and its people. It is based on twenty years of research, fieldwork in Senegal, and friendships with Senegalese.

I would like to thank the following Senegalese for their help and friendship: Ismaila Dia and his family, Abdoulaye Malick Fall, Ibrahima Famara Sagna, Pathé Diagne, Michel Dembelé, Carrie Sembène, and Papa Kane. This book owes a tremendous intellectual debt to scholars who have worked on Senegal and shared their ideas and research with me: Jonathan Barker, Robert Charlick, William Cohen, Lucie Colvin, Clem Cottingham, William Foltz, Wesley Johnson, Martin Klein, Robert Meagher, and Diane Painter. Special thanks go to Professor Martin Klein of the University of Toronto, who carefully went over earlier versions of the manuscript and helped me eliminate some glaring factual errors. For those that remain, I take full responsibility. I would also like to thank USAID officials Arthur Fell and Don Brown for their help and collaboration while I worked with them on consulting assignments in Senegal.

Earlier drafts of this manuscript were typed, edited, and scrutinized by my good friend Louise Rarick. Michel Renaudeau, one of Dakar's best-known photographers and author of several books on Senegal, supplied most of the photographs in the book; Julie Steedman provided the rest. Bob Grody helped with the photos and graphics; Cathryn Lombardi did the maps. Series editor Larry Bowman read several versions of the manuscript and guided it to completion. Susan McRory, Westview copy editor, did a remarkably thorough job of editing the final version of the manuscript. And my wife, Pat, and my children, Michael and Sophia, cheered me on to make sure I finished. To all these collaborators, I owe my thanks.

Sheldon Gellar
Dakar, Senegal

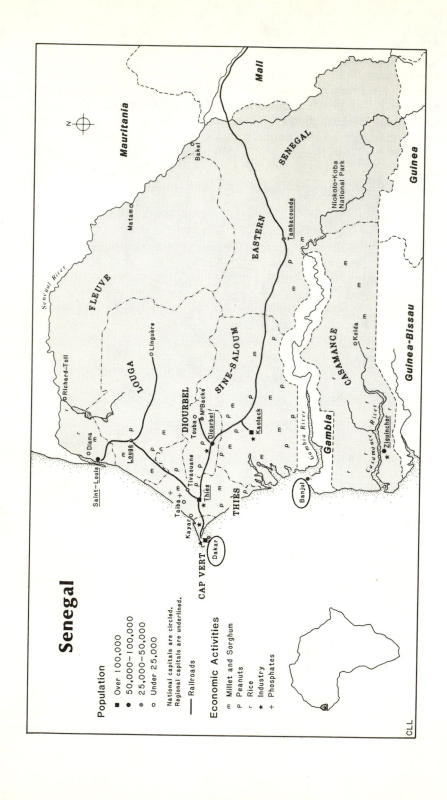

Senegal

Population

- ■ Over 100,000
- ● 50,000–100,000
- ⊙ 25,000–50,000
- ○ Under 25,000

National capitals are circled.
Regional capitals are underlined.

— Railroads

Economic Activities

- m Millet and Sorghum
- p Peanuts
- r Rice
- ★ Industry
- + Phosphates

Mauritania

Mali

SENEGAL

Guinea

Niokolo-Koba
National Park

Guinea-Bissau

⊙ Bakel

Matam ○

FLEUVE

Senegal River

EASTERN

Tambacounda ⊙

○ Richard-Toll

LOUGA

○ Linguère

SINE-SALOUM

CASAMANCE

○ Kolda

Gambia

Gambia River

DIOURBEL

○ Touba
⊙ MBacké
Diourbel ★

Louga ⊙

■ Kaolack ★

Casamance River

Ziguinchor ⊙ ★

○ Diama

Saint-Louis ■

Tivaouane ○

Taiba + m
Kayar ○

Thiès ■ ★

THIES

Banjul ●

CAP VERT

Dakar ■ ★

CLL

1

The Historical Background

Modern Senegal's national development has been profoundly affected by its strategic location and dual vocation as both a Sahelian and an Atlantic country. Sahelian Senegal's long involvement in the trans-Saharan trade exposed it to the strong Islamic traditions of North Africa. Thus, more than a millennium ago the peoples inhabiting the banks of the Senegal River were among the first in West Africa to embrace Islam. And because of its proximity to Western Europe and the New World, Atlantic Senegal became one of the first areas to develop direct commercial ties with Europe, more than five centuries ago, and to send large numbers of slaves to the New World. Senegal's geography has brought its people into close contact with North Africa and the West and made Senegal a crossroads where Black African, Islamic, and European civilizations have met, clashed, and blended. Today, Senegal plays an active role on the world scene as a bridge between Africa and the West and also as an Islamic nation with strong ties to the Muslim world—two roles that Senegalese have been playing for many centuries. Although Islamic and European influences have done much to shape modern Senegal, the Senegalese people also remain deeply attached to traditional Black African values and world views.

PRECOLONIAL SENEGAL

Little is known about the origins of the peoples who now inhabit modern Senegal—the Wolof, Serer, Lebu, Tukolor, Fulbe, Sarakollé, Mandinka, and Diola—or how and when they first arrived in the region. Senegalese historian and cultural nationalist Cheikh Anta Diop has argued that most of Senegal's peoples originated in the Nile River valley and then emigrated to West Africa.[1] Diop based his theory on similarities between the language and culture of Ancient Egypt and those found in Senegal and other parts of West Africa. Although this is an interesting theory, there is little concrete historical evidence to corroborate Diop's hypothesis.

1

While Europe was passing through the Middle Ages, precolonial Senegal had already organized into chiefdoms and larger political units patterned on the Sudanic state model,[2] which flourished in West Africa during the ascendancy of the mighty Ghana and Mali empires. In the Sudanic state system, a dominant ruling lineage usually established its hegemony over other peoples through conquest. Power derived from control over people rather than territory. Because land was plentiful then, the ruler was more concerned with exacting tribute from as many villages and social groups as possible than with exercising direct political sovereignty over a given territory. At the local level, villages, towns, and social groups that were incorporated into the dominant political unit enjoyed a considerable measure of autonomy as long as they acknowledged the authority of the ruling lineage, paid their taxes, provided men for public works and military service, and extended hospitality to state officials passing through. Revolts were frequent, and territorial boundaries expanded and contracted with the rise and decline of the military prowess of the ruling lineage. The political capitals of Sudanic states usually were not fixed but were located wherever the ruler decided to establish his court.

Tekrur, a densely populated kingdom situated in the middle Senegal River valley, was one of the oldest and most prominent of Senegal's precolonial African states.[3] Thanks to its strategic location reaching to the edge of the desert, Tekrur prospered from the trans-Saharan trade between North and West Africa, which involved gold and slaves moving north and cowries, salt, and weapons coming south. During the eleventh century, Tekrur's Tukulor ruler, War Jabi, came under the influence of Muslim traders and missionaries from North Africa and converted to Islam. The great majority of the Tukulor people soon followed War Jabi's example, and the Tukulor became the first major Senegalese ethnic group to embrace Islam en masse. From Tekrur arose the Almoravid movement, which swept through Morocco and Spain during the latter third of the eleventh century. Over the years, Tekrur became a training ground for Muslim clerics and missionaries operating throughout the area of modern Senegal and West Africa.

During the thirteenth century, Tekrur became a vassal state of the powerful Mandinka Mali Empire to the east. At the same time, the Wolof were being unified under the leadership of the legendary Ndiadiane N'Diaye. After the Wolof of Djolof chose N'Diaye as their ruler (bourba), he conquered the Wolof states of Walo, Cayor, and Baol and united them to form the Djolof Empire toward the end of the thirteenth century. Eventually the Djolof Empire extended its dominion to include the predominantly Serer kingdoms of Sine and Saloum.

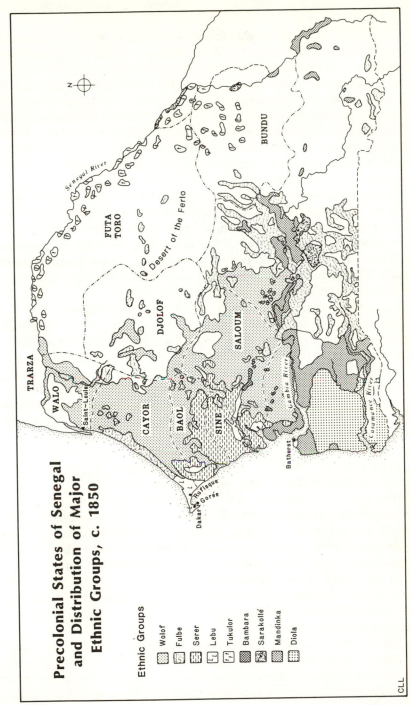

Precolonial States of Senegal and Distribution of Major Ethnic Groups, c. 1850

Ethnic Groups

Wolof
Fulbe
Serer
Lebu
Tukulor
Bambara
Sarakollé
Mandinka
Diola

TRARZA
WALO
CAYOR
BAOL
SINE
SALOUM
DJOLOF
FUTA TORO
BUNDU
Desert of the Ferlo

Senegal River
Gambia River
Casamance River

Saint-Louis
Dakar
Rufisque
Gorée
Bathurst

CLL

Figure 1.1

Although exposed to Islamic influences through Muslim clerics, traders, and court advisers, the Djolof Empire, unlike Tekrur, resisted Islamization and most of its leaders and people remained firmly attached to their traditional religious practices. The Djolof Empire reached its peak during the fifteenth century, when it controlled much of modern Senegal's heartland north of the Gambia River. The empire disintegrated during the second half of the sixteenth century when Baol, Cayor, Walo, Sine, and Saloum broke away to establish their own independent kingdoms. Although the original core state of Djolof survived, it never recaptured its former glory.

Senegal's state structures and social patterns were comparatively stable by the end of the sixteenth century. Most of Senegal's peoples lived in highly stratified societies based primarily on blood relationships. Precolonial Senegalese society was divided into three main social categories: freemen, servile artisan castes, and slaves. Some scholars estimate that as much as one-half to two-thirds of the population were slaves.[4] Less than 10 percent were artisans.

The main characteristic shared by freemen, including royalty and the poorest commoner, was their agricultural vocation and strong attachment to the land. Members of the royal lineages were at the top of the social hierarchy of freemen. Only men with royal blood could aspire to the succession. (Blood lines tended to be traced from the mother's side.) The nobility consisted of those families related to the royal lineages by birth, marriage, and tradition; to local chiefs; and to prominent military commanders. The commoners were freemen who had no royal or noble blood and most were peasants.

There were sharp differences in social status between freemen and the servile castes. Artisans constituted the majority of precolonial Senegal's casted population and supplied most of the goods and services required by a preindustrial agrarian society. The most prominent caste occupations, in descending order of status, were jewelers, blacksmiths, weavers, leather-workers, and *griots*, who were the musicians, praise-singers, and guardians of oral tradition. Occupations were inherited, and intermarriage rarely took place outside of the caste. Casted women shared the status of their spouses and often practiced similar occupations. Despite their inferior social status, casted Africans frequently enjoyed higher standards of living than the average free peasant eking out a hard existence from the soil.

Slaves occupied the bottom rung of society. There were considerable differences in status and treatment among the various categories of slaves. Domestic slaves, i.e., those born into slavery in the household of their master, generally could not be sold. Unlike chattel slaves in the New World, domestic slaves in Senegal, although obliged to work for their masters, were usually given some land of their own to farm and were permitted to marry and raise families. Trade slaves, on the other hand, had no rights. Trade slaves were usually captured in war and sold before they could form any permanent ties with the local community. Crown slaves constituted a third category of slaves. The less fortunate ones performed the most grueling and dangerous forms of manual labor; others served in the ruler's household; and many were recruited into the ruler's army.

The warrior crown slaves (*ceddo*) were a special class. Despite their lowly slave status, many *ceddo* were absorbed into the nobility because of their military prowess. A warrior slave could become a general, lead the ruler's armies, and acquire great wealth and own other slaves. As a group, the *ceddo*, like the Roman Praetorian Guard, often played a decisive role in determining who would rule by supporting or opposing rival claimants for the crown.

The power and prestige of rulers depended largely upon the number of warriors and clients they could maintain in their personal entourages. Rulers were expected to be generous and even extravagant in rewarding their followers. In return, they could count upon their entourage's personal loyalty and devotion. A ruler's entourage cut across class, caste, and kinship lines and included members drawn from all segments of society. Rulers needed warriors to fight their battles, *griots* to sing their praises and mock their enemies, courtiers to provide good counsel and service, skilled artisans to fabricate weapons and luxuries, and slaves to work their fields and mines and serve in their households.

Precolonial Senegal was by no means homogeneous in social organization. Caste lines and slavery, for example, were less developed among the Serer and Diola than among the Tukolor, Wolof, and Mandinka. The Diola and other ethnic groups in the Casamance region usually had less complex and relatively more egalitarian political units than those found in the north. The status of women also was usually higher in the Casamance, where men and women shared agricultural duties.

The peoples of Senegal began to trade with Europe with the arrival of the Portuguese in the mid-fifteenth century. Until the end of the sixteenth century, the Senegambian region was the largest supplier of slaves to Europe.[5] During the seventeenth century, Europeans began to turn their attention to more densely populated areas of West and Central Africa in their quest for slaves to work the sugar plantations of the New World. However, Senegambia remained an important source of slaves, exporting an average of 2,000 to 3,500 slaves a year until the end of the eighteenth century.

The rise of the Atlantic slave trade and the heightened competition for slaves to export spurred warfare within the Senegambian region, disrupted food production, and often brought misery and famine to the masses. The constant warfare was accompanied by a marked increase in the size and power of the warrior class; a widening gulf between nobles and warriors on the one hand and the peasants, who were the main victims of slave raids, on the other hand; and *ceddo* plundering of the countryside. The intensification of the slave trade in the Senegal River region during the latter half of the seventeenth century gave rise to a popular but unsuccessful movement (1673–1677) led by Muslim clerics, or marabouts. The movement was a revolt against the tyranny of the slave-trading traditional aristocracy, who put down the revolt with the help of firearms supplied by the French from Saint Louis.[6]

The French had originally come to Senegal to reap the benefits of the Atlantic slave trade and to assert France's position as a major European naval power. They gained a solid foothold in Senegal after establishing a fort and trading post at Saint Louis in 1659 and driving the Dutch from the isle of Gorée in 1677.

EUROPEAN IMPERIALISM AND ISLAM

British and French rivalry for empire and control over West African trade during the eighteenth century often pitted these two powers against each other in the Senegambian region. France controlled Saint Louis and Gorée, and the British had established themselves further south near the mouth of the Gambia River. Neither power was strong enough to drive the other out of the region or to penetrate the interior, which remained under African rule. Their presence, however, laid the groundwork for the eventual partition of the Senegambian region into the British colony of the Gambia and the French colony of Senegal in the late nineteenth century.

The growing imperialist rivalry between France and Britain also coincided with a militant Islamic revival in Senegal.[7] In 1776 a group of Tukulor marabouts led a successful revolution that overthrew the Denianké dynasty, rulers of Futa Toro since the sixteenth century. After establishing a theocratic oligarchy, the leaders of the clerical party began to send missionaries throughout Senegal and to develop close ties with other resurgent Islamic movements in Guinea and elsewhere in West Africa.

During the mid-nineteenth century, Tukulor clerics from Futa Toro led many of the jihads, or holy wars, that sought to overturn pagan rulers and create Muslim theocratic states in the region. The most eminent of the Muslim clerical warriors was Al Haj Umar Tall. While on pilgrimage to Mecca in the 1820s, Tall was initiated into the Tijaniyya brotherhood, an organization that had been founded in Fez (Morocco) by Ahmad al-

Tijani in the late eighteenth century. As the appointed Tijani khalife (caliph) for the western Sudan, Tall acquired a large following after visiting the major West African Muslim courts at Kanem, Sokoto, Macina, and Futa Djallon. In 1852 he organized an army recruited largely from his native Futa Toro and made preparations for a jihad to build a Tijani Islamic empire. After conquering vast stretches of pagan and Muslim territory from Medina to the Niger Bend, Tall moved to extend his power to Senegal. There he came into conflict with the French, who were themselves embarking on a campaign to extend their power.

France's program for expansion began shortly after Major Louis Faidherbe was named governor of French Senegal in 1854. Faidherbe first launched a successful military campaign to subjugate the Moors of Trarza, who controlled the lucrative gum trade on both sides of the Senegal River, and then in 1855 he annexed Walo, which became the first indigenous state in Senegal to come directly under French rule. Next Faidherbe built forts at Matam, Bakel, and other points along the Senegal River to ensure French control and to stop the westward advance of Tall. By the end of 1859, several efforts by Tall to dislodge the French had failed, and the Tukulor leader once again turned his attention east, where he consolidated his hold over a vast empire before dying in battle in 1864. Tall's Islamic reform movement was the first to come into open conflict with European imperialist ambitions in West Africa, and Tall himself became a rallying point for African resistance to the French.

Other Islamic reformers followed Tall's example and clashed with pagan states and peoples resisting conversion to Islam as well as with the French. One of the most prominent of these warrior reformers was Ma Ba, a Tukulor cleric and disciple of Al Haj Umar Tall, who in 1861 launched a holy war and religious revolution against the pagan Mandinka chiefdoms and states along the Gambia River. Ma Ba's religious wars pitted the party of the marabouts against the traditional rulers and ceddo. By the mid 1860s, Ma Ba's forces also controlled much of Saloum and Djolof, and he had converted several prominent Wolof leaders to Islam, including Lat Dior of Cayor and Alboury N'Diaye of Djolof, who both played major roles in the Islamization of their home states and led the resistance against the French. Ma Ba died in 1867 during a decisive battle in which the pagan Serer state of Sine dealt a devastating defeat to Ma Ba's forces, temporarily halting the rapid advance of Islam in the region.

Meanwhile, the French were busy extending their control over the Senegal River from Saint Louis to Bakel and gaining a foothold on the mainland further south. In 1857, the French established a military post in the Lebu village of Dakar and gradually acquired control over the rest of the Cap Vert Peninsula. They then built several forts along the coast and sent troops and gunboats to the interior to protect French commerce and affirm France's hegemony over the inland states. Resistance to the French conquest and occupation of African soil was widespread in Senegal. In many areas, particularly in the Wolof states, Islam became a catalyst for armed resistance. After the final defeat of the Wolof armies and the death of Lat Dior in 1886, the French were able to exercise direct control over most of Senegal with the exception of the Casamance, where the Diola and other ethnic groups continued to fight the French into the twentieth century.

The French conquest of Senegal had the greatest impact on the Wolof, whose military defeat was accompanied by the dismemberment of their states and tremendous social upheavals. The defeat of the Wolof nobility and the disbanding of the *ceddo* class destroyed the power and prestige of the "pagan party" that had earlier resisted Islamization. At this point, the Wolof masses turned for guidance to holy men like Amadou Bamba, who founded the Mouride brotherhood, and Malick Sy, founder of Senegal's most prominent Tijaniyya religious dynasty. The Islamization of the Wolof toward the end of the nineteenth century and their integration into Muslim brotherhoods led by venerated marabouts created new authority structures that initially aroused the suspicion of the French, who were attempting to impose the authority of the colonial state.

Social structures underwent fewer dramatic changes in Futa Toro, Sine, and the Casamance. In Futa Toro, the French named members of the *grandes familles* who had collaborated with the French to be the canton chiefs (*chefs de canton*) in the colonial system; in Sine, the pagan Serer were allowed to retain their traditional political structures for a while. However, in all instances the French eventually dismantled the conquered African states, divided them into smaller units, and superimposed French administrative structures on them.

Just as precolonial Senegal had been one of the first areas in West Africa to develop commercial ties with Europe and participate in the Atlantic slave trade, in the nineteenth century Senegal became one of the first areas in West Africa to become integrated into the modern industrial world capitalist system following the demise of the Atlantic slave trade. Senegal entered this system in 1840 when it sent a shipload of peanuts to France, where the cargo was used to produce cooking oil and soap for European consumers. Within a few decades, the peanut trade, or *traite*, had become the cornerstone of the economy for many Africans, and peanuts had become Senegal's main export, supplanting gum and slaves.

Until the mid-nineteenth century, trading relationships between Europe and the African states of precolonial Senegal were based on more or less mutual reciprocity. African rulers and chiefs were able to improve their terms of trade by taking advantage of the national and commercial rivalries among the European powers trading in the Senegambian region. Moreover, the Africans were able to levy customs duties on imports and exports passing through their territory. Faidherbe's military campaigns were initially instigated primarily for economic reasons. They were intended to establish a French presence on the mainland that could protect French commerce and end African control over inland trade routes and trading posts. The military campaigns that followed the Berlin Congress of 1884–1885 had a far more ambitious aim—the establishment of French sovereignty over Senegal and other African territories destined to become part of republican France's vast West African empire.

THE COLONIAL ERA (1885–1945)

Senegal's colonial experience has profoundly affected its modern national development. Colonial rule in Senegal, as elsewhere in Africa, was essentially a system of political, economic, and cultural domination forcibly imposed by a technologically advanced foreign minority on an indigenous majority. As a system, colonialism justified itself largely through ideologies that asserted the superiority of the colonizer and the inferiority of the colonized. France defended its acquisition of colonies on the grounds of a "civilizing mission" that would bring peace, prosperity, and the benefits of French civilization to the "backward and primitive" peoples fortunate enough to come under French rule. The colonial situation permitted France to deny its colonial subjects the political and civil rights that its own people enjoyed at home and to make policy largely on the basis of what was good for France or for French nationals living in the colonies.

Senegal was the only colony in Black Africa in which France attempted to apply assimilationist ideals.[8] Thus, Senegal had its own territorial assembly (Conseil General), municipal councils patterned on those found in metropolitan France, and a representative who sat in the French Chamber of Deputies in Paris. Africans born in the urban communes of Dakar, Gorée, Rufisque, and Saint Louis were granted full citizenship rights. This meant that male African "citizens" from the "Four Communes" could participate in modern electoral politics, hold political office (if they met certain educational qualifications), and escape the servitude imposed on their less fortunate countrymen in the interior, who were regarded as "subjects" by the French colonial authorities. The Senegalese citizens were a tiny privileged minority, constituting less than 5 percent of the total population throughout the colonial period. In addition to enjoying the benefits of French citizenship, Senegalese citizens also had greater access to Western education and employment in modern economic activities.

The location of the federal capital of French West Africa in Senegal was another sign of that colony's privileged status. Created in 1895, the French West African Federation was headed by a French governor-general. From 1895 to 1902, when the federal capital moved to Dakar, the governor of Senegal also served as governor-general. However, in 1902, the two positions were separated and the powers of the governor-general increased. The governor-general, housed in his luxurious colonial palace, soon became the major symbol of France's imperial presence. Dakar itself was transformed into an imperial city containing the most advanced administrative and social services in French Black Africa. And Senegal enjoyed preeminence over the federation's other colonies—French Soudan, Mauritania, Guinea, Ivory Coast, Upper Volta, Niger, and Dahomey.

Colonial Senegal was divided into two distinct political and administrative entities that reflected the sharp differences in status between the citizens of the Four Communes and the subjects of rural Senegal. Although economically dominated by the French, the Four Communes had a vibrant political life based on competitive electoral politics and was one of the rare areas in colonial Africa where Europeans and Western-educated Afro-Europeans and Africans could engage in politics on an equal basis. Rural Senegal, on the other hand, was governed along more autocratic lines by colonial administrators.[9]

Outside the Four Communes, the country was divided into fifteen administrative districts (cercles) each headed by a French commandant whose military title accurately reflected the authoritarian character of his role. The colonial system of "native justice" (indigénat) gave the commandant the right to arrest and jail without trial African subjects for such offenses as not paying taxes, unwillingness to serve on forced-labor crews, and not showing the proper respect for French authority. Commandants could also impose collective fines on entire villages and expropriate village land by administrative fiat. As representatives of the colonial state, they were responsible only to the French colonial governor of Senegal, whose policies they carried out.

The main administrative unit below the cercle was the canton. Each cercle was divided into several cantons headed by African canton chiefs named by the colonial administration and directly incorporated into the colonial bureaucracy. Although the French often chose as canton chiefs local leaders with high traditional status, in some areas they chose outsiders or people of low status who knew how to read and write French and who enjoyed the confidence of the colonial authorities. Canton chiefs had the unpopular tasks of collecting taxes and recruiting men for labor gangs. Some abused their authority by extorting money from the people in their districts. Their dependence upon the French colonial administration for their position and their subordinate rank in the colonial bureaucracy undermined their legitimacy with the rural masses, who regarded them primarily as agents of the French.

The great disparity in colonial status between citizens and subjects gave rise to two markedly different styles of political leadership. In the communes, the prototype of the political leader was the urbane, Western-educated Senegalese intellectual; in the countryside, it was the marabout.

Mastery of the French language and familiarity with French culture and institutions were prerequisites for political leadership in the Four Communes. The Western-educated Senegalese citizens who were actively involved in colonial electoral politics clearly identified with the egalitarian ideals embodied in the French Revolution and the Declaration of the Rights of Man. Members of an "auxiliary" elite playing a subordinate role within the colonial system, they were more concerned with ending racial discrimination than with winning political independence. They wanted equality with the French and worked hard to make French assimilationist ideals a reality in Senegal. Senegalese intellectuals followed international events and political developments in France and Europe very closely, a trait that remains characteristic of the Senegalese political elite.

In 1914, Blaise Diagne, a colonial customs official, became Senegal's first Black African deputy in the French parliament. Diagne held the seat until his death in 1934. His election marked the ascendancy of Black African leadership in Senegalese politics, which had been previously dominated by French and Afro-French (métis) politicians.[10] By 1920, the majority of local elective offices were also in African hands.

Blaise Diagne's long and brilliant career as deputy was marked by several major political developments that became integral features of Senegalese colonial politics: (1) the active involvement of the Senegalese deputy in metropolitan politics; (2) the polarization and personalization of party politics around the figure of the deputy; and (3) the growing involvement of Muslim religious authorities in electoral politics.

In 1915 and 1916, Diagne offered to recruit Black African troops throughout French West Africa to fight for France in World War I in exchange for legislation that permanently guaranteed the rights of French citizenship to his African constituents in the Four Communes in the face of efforts by colonial administrators and French residents to disenfranchise them. During the early 1920s, Diagne became a leading spokesman for the Bordeaux trading companies that then controlled Senegal's colonial export economy and allied himself with the so-called Colonial

iii. DAKAR — Les élections au Sénégal

Figure 1.2. Election time in colonial Dakar (from a colonial postcard collection). (Photo by Michel Renaudeau)

Party, a group of French deputies and senators promoting metropolitan colonial economic interests. Regarded as a dangerous radical by the French in 1914, Diagne by the end of his career had become a pillar of the colonial establishment, enjoying the confidence of French colonial officials and the French business community.

While Diagne was championing assimilationist policies and defending the rights of the citizens, the subjects in the interior were attempting to adjust to colonial rule. Unlike the westernized citizens in the communes whose mastery of French language and culture was an instrument for political, social, and economic advancement, the subjects had little reason to embrace French culture or French political institutions, which they saw expressed primarily in the form of an autocratic colonial bureaucracy. The decline of chiefly authority and the peaceful spread of Islam throughout much of Senegal was accompanied by the rise of Muslim brotherhoods, which provided a new form of political leadership for the rural masses. At first, the French sought to stifle the growing influence of the marabouts by deporting popular leaders like Amadou Bamba, who underwent exile twice, first to Gabon (1895–1902) and then to Mauritania (1903–1907). However, Bamba's exile made him even more of a hero to the rural Wolof masses, and his return from exile was marked with great celebration.

Toward the end of the first decade of the century, the French colonial authorities in Senegal reversed their anti-Islamic policies and moved to reach a modus vivendi with Muslim religious leaders willing to preach acceptance of the authority of the colonial state. Prominent Muslim leaders like Amadou Bamba, Malick Sy, and Seydou Nourou Tall realized that they could not drive the French out by military force and thus decided to make their peace with the colonial regime in exchange for a free hand in preaching and organizing their followers within the framework of the Muslim brotherhoods. During World War I, many prominent marabouts demonstrated their loyalty to France by collaborating with the colonial authorities in recruiting African troops for the war effort.

While the marabouts made their peace with the colonial state, they kept their distance from westernizing influences. Thus, the marabouts discouraged their followers from attending French schools and created their own network of Koranic schools and pioneer youth colonies. For their part, the French kept Catholic missionaries out of Muslim areas. As a result, Catholic missions in the interior were restricted primarily to territories occupied by the then predominantly pagan Serer and Diola populations. Even there, Islam advanced more rapidly than Christianity.

Although the marabouts resisted cultural assimilation, they were very much involved in Senegalese colonial politics, offering their support and that of their following to Senegalese citizen politicians in exchange for certain favors — e.g., government subsidies for building mosques, jobs and trading licenses for their faithful followers, and redress against abuses perpetuated by the colonial administration. The Mourides, for example, financed much of Blaise Diagne's successful 1914 campaign for deputy in the hope that Diagne would defend them against administrative persecution.

In addition to preaching obedience to the colonial authorities, the marabouts urged their *talibés* (disciples) to grow peanuts for the market in the new areas where they were settling. The French were delighted with this practice, as it promoted the expansion of peanut production, the foundation of the colonial economy. Because of its interest in extending peanut production, the colonial administration granted many prominent Mouride and Tijani marabouts large tracts of land that became peanut estates and often supported the marabouts in their disputes with Fulbe herders, who were fighting to retain control over their traditional grazing lands that were being taken over by the peanut farmers.

It would be difficult to exaggerate the significance of the rise of the peanut export economy in shaping the contours of Senegal's economic life.[11] Peanut exports began before the advent of colonial rule, but French colonial investments in ports, roads, and railroads facilitated the rapid expansion of peanut production by lowering transportation costs and making it easier to evacuate peanuts from the interior. In 1885 the Dakar–Saint Louis railroad was opened–the first railroad in West Africa. Between 1885 and 1914 peanut production increased from 45,000 tons to 300,000 tons[12] and followed the eastward expansion of the Dakar-Niger railroad toward Tambacounda. The heart of the peanut zones lay within the boundaries of what had been formerly the states of Cayor, Baol, Walo, Sine, and Saloum. The railroads set the geographical boundaries of commercial agriculture, as 93 percent of Senegalese peanuts were produced in regions serviced by the Dakar–Saint Louis and Dakar-Niger railroads.[13] Conversely, regions like Futa Toro, Eastern Senegal, and much of the Casamance, which had no railroads to link them to the coast, remained largely outside the cash-crop economy.

The pattern of commercialization during this period of rapid economic growth was accompanied by the development of three distinct but interdependent economic and geographic sectors in Senegal: (1) a modern sector concentrated in the federal capital of Dakar, where the major import-export houses and colonial banks had their headquarters, and to a lesser extent in Saint Louis, Rufisque, and the larger towns in the interior; (2) a cash-crop sector that corresponded with the main peanut-producing regions; and (3) a predominantly subsistence sector devoid of cash crops, which encompassed the so-called peripheral regions and exported labor to the towns and peanut zones.

By World War I, the foundations of Senegal's export economy had been solidly established and the colony's prosperity was inextricably linked to the peanut. Growing peanuts for the market became the main source of cash income for most of Senegal's rural population. Peanuts sparked the growth of trade and generated more revenues for the colonial state. By the end of the 1930s, nearly two-thirds of Senegal's rural populations were engaged in peanut farming; more than 600,000 tons of peanuts were produced in a good year.

Although its peanut production and exports made Senegal the wealthiest colony in French West Africa, the peanut economy was, at best, a mixed blessing for Senegal's African population.[14] In the first place, the expatriate import-export companies and colonial banks, which dominated the peanut trade, derived most of the benefits. Second, during the interwar years (1919–1939), Senegalese peanut farmers suffered from a sharp deterioration in their terms of trade as peanut prices dropped relative to the prices of the goods they bought. Third, many farmers went heavily into debt when crops failed or when peanut prices fell, and they found it increasingly difficult to get out of debt. Fourth, the expansion of peanut production often took place at the expense of traditional food crops. Fifth, French colonial policy, with its heavy emphasis

Figure 1.3. A typical colonial peanut trading post in Louga (from a colonial postcard collection). (Photo by Michel Renaudeau)

on peanut production, neglected the development of the agricultural potential of the regions lying outside the main peanut zones and locked Senegal into an increasingly unremunerative single-crop economy. Finally, the French did little to improve the productivity of Senegalese farmers.

Dakar's special status as the administrative and commercial capital of French West Africa was another major factor shaping colonial Senegal's economic development. The French built up Dakar as an imperial city from which France would govern and develop its West African empire. Following the transfer of the federal capital from Saint Louis to Dakar in 1902, Dakar soon became the center for French West Africa's most advanced government services, providing secondary schools, hospitals, and research facilities to serve the entire federation. At the same time, the French spent heavily to modernize Dakar and make it the hub of economic life in the French West African Federation. Improvements in port facilities quickly transformed Dakar into French West Africa's most important port. The construction of the Dakar-Niger railroad connecting Senegal to French Soudan (now Mali) spurred peanut production and made Dakar a major entrepôt for trade between France and French Soudan. Attracted by Dakar's modern infrastructure and ur-

ban amenities, most major French and other European trading companies doing business in French West Africa set up their overseas headquarters in the federal capital. Shortly afterward, Dakar replaced Saint
Louis, the once proud territorial capital, as Senegal's largest urban
center. By the end of the 1930s, its population had soared to more than
100,000, including a French population of nearly 10,000, the largest
European community in all West Africa.

The Lebanese were another important non-African group active in
Senegal's colonial development. First coming to Senegal toward the end
of the nineteenth century, they helped extend the boundaries of the
peanut economy by offering cash for peanuts and operating in areas
previously neglected by the French. Because of their willingness to accept lower standards of living, Lebanese traders had a competitive edge
over French and Senegalese middlemen.

The 1930s was a difficult and turbulent period in Senegal's colonial
history. Drought and the Great Depression brought drastic declines in
the living standards of Senegal's rural population when world peanut
prices and domestic peanut production plummeted. Although French
protectionist policies contributed to the recovery of peanut production
by guaranteeing markets for Senegalese peanuts in the metropole, rural
living standards remained depressed as local peanut prices stayed well
below predepression levels. During this period, French colonial banks
and import-export houses reinforced their hold over the Senegalese
economy while the Lebanese became the main intermediaries in the
peanut trade.

In the political arena, Galendou Diouf, Blaise Diagne's successor as
deputy (1934–1940), also aligned himself with the Dakar-based colonial
establishment. His main opponent was Lamine Guèye, Senegal's first
Black African lawyer and founder of the Parti Socialiste Sénégalaise
(Senegalese Socialist party – PSS), which established formal links with
the French Socialist party (SFIO) in the metropole.[15] Although he was
defeated in 1936 by Diouf, Guèye's star rose with the coming to power in
France of the Socialist-led Popular Front government (1936–1938), which
restricted the use of forced labor in the colonies, gave Africans the right
to form their own trade unions, and simplified naturalization procedures
for Africans seeking to become French citizens. Taking advantage of the
more liberal political climate, Guèye began to organize Socialist party
units in the interior and to encourage Western-educated subjects to play
a greater role in Senegalese politics, which had previously been limited
almost exclusively to the confines of the Four Communes. The demise of
the Popular Front in 1938 brought an abrupt halt to colonial reform and a
reversal of Guèye's political fortunes.

The outbreak of World War II led to a marked deterioration in the political and economic status of Senegal's African population.[16] As in 1914, France called upon Senegal and its other African colonies to provide troops and materials for the war effort. After the fall of France in 1940, the reactionary Vichy regime abolished Senegal's representative assemblies, outlawed all trade unions, and denied Senegal's African citizens the prerogatives and rights of French citizenship. Most Senegalese suffered under the Vichy regime as the colonial administration stepped up its use of forced labor and confiscation of African stocks of rice, millet, and other raw materials. After taking its tribute for the war effort, the colonial administration left little for the Senegalese.

In November 1942, French colonial officials in Senegal rallied to General Charles de Gaulle, leader of the Free French forces. Despite the elimination of Vichy rule, economic conditions remained harsh for Africans, and the French did not restore Senegalese political institutions until the end of the war.

THE ROAD TO INDEPENDENCE (1945-1960)

With the victory of the Allies in sight, General de Gaulle organized a conference to discuss the future of France's Black African colonies. The Brazzaville Conference (November–December 1944), held in the capital of French Equatorial Africa, formally committed the metropole to postwar colonial reform and marked the end of the old autocratic colonial era. General de Gaulle and the colonial officials who dominated the conference defined reform largely in terms of the metropole's making a greater effort to promote the social and economic well-being of its overseas populations and granting them a larger voice in the administration of their territories. The Brazzaville Conference had little to say about political reform and pointedly excluded independence as a possible option for France's Black African colonies.

In 1946, overseas African deputies worked closely with metropolitan deputies from the French left to push through reforms that drastically altered the relationships between France and her colonies. These reforms included: (1) the abolition of forced labor and the *indigénat*; (2) the elimination of distinctions in status between citizens and subjects; (3) the extension of the suffrage and greater Black African representation in metropolitan assemblies; and (4) the creation of the Economic and Social Development Investment Fund (FIDES) to subsidize overseas development programs.

A distinctive feature of postwar Sengal's political development was the great involvement of Senegal's political leaders in metropolitan and inter-African politics.[17] While he was a deputy (1945-1951), Lamine Guèye was one of the most influential Africans in the French parliament.

As leader of the group of African deputies and member of the executive bureau of the French Socialist party, Guèye gave his name to the 1946 law that obliterated the distinction between citizen and subject. He also championed legislation to provide equal pay for equal work for African civil servants, who had been subjected to lower pay scales than their French counterparts throughout the colonial era. His influence began to wane both at home and in Paris after the French Socialists with whom he was allied lost control of the Overseas Ministry.

In 1948, Léopold Sédar Senghor, Senegal's second deputy and a protégé of Guèye, broke away from the Socialists and formed a new political party, the Bloc Démocratique Sénégalais (Senegalese Democratic Bloc – BDS). At the same time, Senghor aligned himself with the Catholic-based Mouvement Républicain Populaire (People's Republican Movement – MRP) in France and assumed the leadership of a loose coalition of African parliamentarians called the Indépendants d'Outre-Mer (Overseas Independents – IOM). During the late 1940s and early 1950s, Senghor and the IOM were primarily concerned with economic issues; Senghor himself became one of the most forceful advocates for increasing the volume of FIDES credits and constantly reminded the metropole of its obligation to provide better educational and health facilities for its overseas African populations.

In 1953, Senghor attempted to transform the IOM from a loose parliamentary alliance to a disciplined interterritorial African movement similar to the Rassemblement Démocratique Africain (African Democratic Assembly – RDA), then headed by Felix Houphouët-Boigny of the Ivory Coast. The IOM did not become a powerful interterritorial party as Senghor had hoped, but it did provide him with a platform during the mid-1950s to call for new political arrangements between France and French West Africa in which each African territory would have its own parliament and executive and would become integrated into a French federal republic with a federal parliament and executive in Paris. In October 1954, Senghor proposed that the West African territories join a French federal republic as two separate entities, one with its capital in Dakar (which would include Senegal, Mauritania, French Soudan, and Guinea), and the other with its capital in Abidjan (which would include the Ivory Coast and the rest of the French West African territories).

At home, the 1946 colonial reforms led to major changes in Senegal's political life.[18] In the first place, the extension of the suffrage to the rural population ended the citizens' monopoly of Senegalese politics and greatly enhanced the power and influence of the marabouts. The emergence of the BDS as Senegal's majority party in 1951–1952 was largely due to its capitalizing on the subjects' resentment of the citizens' past privileges and condescending attitudes and its success in winning the support of most of Senegal's prominent Muslim leaders. While remaining strong in the Four Communes, Lamine Guèye's once dominant Socialist party never regained power again because of its lack of electoral support in the countryside. A second major development was the appearance of trade unionists, Marxist intellectuals, and university students as important actors in Senegalese politics. Espousing a more nationalistic and radical brand of politics, they tended to regard both the BDS and the Senegalese Socialists as establishment parties too closely wedded to the French. Lacking a mass base, they remained outside the mainstream of Senegalese electoral politics. Third, despite a sharp increase in the size of the French community in Senegal—from 16,500 in 1945 to 38,000 during the 1950s—European participation and involvement in Senegalese politics became virtually nonexistent as few Europeans sought political office. Fourth, French colonial administrators were no longer a law unto themselves and became increasingly subjected to pressures exerted by Senegal's political leaders.

The postwar colonial reforms, although they accelerated the pace of political decolonization, did little to alter the structures of Senegal's peanut-based export economy or transfer economic power from the French to the Senegalese. French firms and businessmen still controlled the peanut trade and the more advanced sectors of the economy and continued to import skilled workers and middle-level managers from the metropole rather than upgrade the skills of the African work force. As in the past, Dakar received a disproportionate share of French investments in Senegal, which were aimed at modernizing its administrative infrastructure, port facilities, and transportation networks and transforming the Cap Vert Peninsula into a major industrial pole serving French West Africa and the metropole. The priority given to Cap Vert widened still further the economic gap between Dakar and the countryside. And despite some modest improvements in wages and peanut prices due to vigorous trade union activities and metropolitan subsidizing of peanut prices, living standards remained low for most African farmers and workers during the postwar era.

As nationalist demands for independence grew, the French attempted to dampen them by initiating the Loi-Cadre of 1956, which set the stage for self-government by broadening the powers of the territorial assemblies and providing for an African-controlled government in each territory. At this time, the BDS, led by Senghor and Mamadou Dia, his trusted political lieutenant, was moving to the left. When several prominent Marxist intellectuals joined the BDS, the party changed its name to the Bloc Populaire Sénégalais (Senegalese People's Bloc—BPS) to reflect its turn to the left. After the BPS defeated Lamine Guèye's Socialists in the March 1957 territorial elections, Mamadou Dia assumed the reins of

Senegal's first territorial government. In April 1958 the Socialists merged with the BPS to form the Union Progressiste Sénégalaise (Senegalese Progressive Union – UPS).

General de Gaulle's return to power following the May 13, 1958, uprising in Algeria created a new political situation. De Gaulle held out three options for France's Black African territories: (1) total integration with France, an option that no one took seriously; (2) political autonomy as self-governing republics within the framework of a French Community dominated by France, which would continue to be responsible for foreign affairs, defense, financial and monetary matters, and higher education – the option preferred by de Gaulle; and (3) immediate independence.

The latter two options were intensely debated in Senegal as throughout the French West African Federation. Militant trade unionists, students, and the left wing of the UPS wanted immediate independence. On the other hand, Senegal's marabouts were united in their opposition to independence because they thought that the radicals might possibly take power and launch a campaign to undermine the marabouts' authority. Fearing the defection of the marabouts and economic reprisals by France, Senghor finally decided to ask the UPS to reject immediate independence in favor of self-government within the framework of the French Community. After a stormy debate, the radical wing of the UPS walked out and formed a new party to campaign for immediate independence in the September 28, 1958, referendum, in which the territories were asked to maintain or sever their formal ties with France. A yes vote meant opting for self-government within a French Community dominated by France; a no vote meant opting for immediate independence and the possibility of seeing all French aid terminated abruptly. Despite strong nationalist support for a no vote in Dakar, Saint Louis, and the Casamance, the yes vote carried the day in Senegal.

Guinea was the only Black African territory to vote for immediate independence in the referendum. Despite reprisals by France, Guinea's bold decision set a precedent and encouraged Senegal and other francophone African states to seek full independence from France. In 1959 Senegal began negotiations with France to obtain its independence as a constituent unit of the Mali Federation,[19] which comprised Senegal and the former French Soudan. By the end of 1959, de Gaulle had become resigned to accepting independence as a legitimate option, provided that the former colonies agreed to maintain close political, economic, and cultural ties with France. The Mali Federation formally became independent on April 4, 1960, a date that is still celebrated in Senegal as Independence Day. However, the federation did not last long, primarily because of personal rivalries between Senegalese and Soudanese political leaders and conflicting ideas about the form and future direction that the federation should take. Senegal feared being dominated by its larger neighbor and wanted a loose federation that would permit Senegal to retain its political autonomy and party structures. Senghor also worried about political intrigues between Senegalese and Soudanese politicians to replace him as Senegal's leader and thwart his ambitions to become president of the Mali Federation. The federation broke up on August 22, 1960, when the Senegalese arrested the Soudanese leader, Modibo Keita, in Dakar and shipped him back to Bamako in a sealed railroad car. Immediately afterwards, the Senegalese National Assembly met in emergency session to declare Senegal's secession from the Mali Federation. By the end of September 1960, Senegal had its own constitution and a seat in the United Nations.

NOTES

1. See, for example, *L'Afrique noire pré-Coloniale* [Precolonial Black Africa] (Paris: Présence Africaine, 1960).

2. For an analysis of the Sudanic state system, see J. Spencer Trimingham, *A History of Islam in West Africa* (London: Oxford University Press, 1962), pp. 34–37.

3. For a succinct discussion of the development of Senegal's precolonial African states, see G. Wesley Johnson, Jr., *The Emergence of Black Politics in Senegal: The Struggle for Power in the Four Communes, 1900–1920* (Stanford, Calif.: Stanford University Press, 1971), pp. 7–17.

4. For example, see Philip D. Curtin, *Economic Change in Precolonial Africa: Senegambia in the Era of the Slave Trade* (Madison: University of Wisconsin Press, 1975), p. 36; and Majhemout Diop, *Histoire des classes sociales dans l'Afrique de l'Ouest, Le Sénégal* [History of social classes in West Africa: Senegal] (Paris: François Maspero, 1972), pp. 27–31.

5. For a detailed discussion of the Senegambian slave trade, see Curtin, *Economic Change in Precolonial Africa*, pp. 153–196.

6. See Boubacar Barry, *La Royaume du Waalo: Le Sénégal avant La conquête* [The kingdom of Waalo: Senegal before the Conquest] (Paris: François Maspero, 1972).

7. For some of the best works on the Islamic revival and the advance of French imperialism, see Martin A. Klein, *Islam and Imperialism in Senegal: Sine-Saloum 1847–1914* (Stanford, Calif.: Stanford University Press, 1968); Martin A. Klein, "Social and Economic Factors in the Muslim Revolution in Senegambia," *Journal of African History* 13 (1972): 419–441; and David W. Robinson, *Clerics and Chiefs: The History of Abdul Bokar Kane and the Futa Toro* (New York: Oxford University Press, 1976).

8. For a full discussion of this point, see Michael Crowder, *Senegal: A Study of French Assimilation Policy* (London: Oxford University Press, 1962).

9. For two major studies of the French colonial administration in Africa see Robert Delavignette, *Freedom and Authority in French West Africa* (London: Oxford University Press, 1950); and William B. Cohen, *Rulers of Empire: The French Colonial Service in Africa* (Stanford, Calif.: Stanford University Press, 1971).

10. For a detailed analysis of this important phase in Senegalese colonial politics, see Johnson, *Emergence of Black Politics in Senegal*, pp. 121–219.

11. The most extensive quantitative study of the development of peanut production in Senegal is André Vanhaeverbeke, *Rémuneration du travail et commerce extérieur: Essor d'une economie exportatrice et termes de l'échange des producteurs d'arachides au Sénégal* [Remuneration of labor and foreign trade: Progress of an export economy and the terms of trade of peanut producers in Senegal] (Louvain: Centre de Recherches des Pays en Développement, 1970).

12. All tons are metric.

13. Vanhaeverbeke, *Rémuneration du travail et commerce extérieur*, p. 16.

14. For more on this point, see Sheldon Gellar, *Structural Changes and Colonial Dependancy: Senegal 1885–1945* (Beverly Hills, Calif.: Sage Publications, 1976), pp. 49–66.

15. For more details on Senegalese politics during this period, see Ruth Schachter-Morgenthau, *Political Parties in French-Speaking West Africa* (London: Oxford University Press, 1964), pp. 127–134.

16. See Jean Suret-Canale, *Afrique noire, occidentale et centrale, L'ère coloniale 1900–1945* [West and Central Black Africa, the colonial era, 1900–1945] (Paris: Editions Sociales, 1964), pp. 567–600, for a detailed discussion of the war years (1939–1945).

17. For more on this, see Schachter-Morgenthau, *Political Parties in French-Speaking West Africa*, pp. 32–124; and Edward Mortimer, *France and the Africans, 1944–1960: A Political History* (New York: Walker and Company, 1969).

18. For extensive analyses of postwar Senegalese politics, see Schachter-Morgenthau, *Political Parties in French-Speaking West Africa*, pp. 134–165; Kenneth Robinson, "Senegal," in W.J.K. Mackenzie and Kenneth Robinson, eds., *Five Elections in Africa* (London: Oxford University Press, 1960), pp. 281–390; and Sheldon Gellar, "The Politics of Development in Senegal," Ph.D. dissertation, Columbia University, 1967, pp. 148–228.

19. For the story of the rise and fall of the Mali Federation, see William F. Foltz, *From French West Africa to the Mali Federation* (New Haven, Conn.: Yale University Press, 1965).

2

Government and Politics

One of the most stable and least repressive political regimes on the African continent, Senegal has been spared the ethnic and religious strife that has torn apart other African nations and has avoided the military coups that elsewhere have spelled the demise of civilian rule. Senegal owes much of its political stability to Léopold Sédar Senghor, who led the country during its first two decades of independence. In January 1981, Senghor became the first African head of state to freely leave office before the end of his term. His successor, Abdou Diouf, assumed office after a remarkably smooth and peaceful transition and quickly asserted his authority as an energetic and forceful national leader.

After a long period of single-party rule, Senegal since the mid-1970s has been moving towards a more competitive multiparty system. In 1982 Senegal had eleven opposition political parties representing diverse shades of the political spectrum and a lively and vigorous opposition press. Although still one of the most fascinating experiments in African political democracy, Senegalese democracy is going through a difficult period, beset by harsh economic problems and a militant but fragmented opposition seeking more radical solutions to the country's current woes.

SENEGALESE POLITICS: THE SENGHOR ERA, 1960–1980

Senegalese politics during the long postcolonial Senghor era went through three distinct periods. The first (1960–1963)[1] was characterized by fiercely competitive electoral politics, the consolidation of the UPS's hold over the country, and the emergence of Senghor as Senegal's undisputed national leader. During this period, the UPS went through its gravest internal crisis as a result of a power struggle between President Senghor and Prime Minister Mamadou Dia. The crisis, which divided the party into two camps, reached its peak in mid-December 1962 when a majority of UPS deputies in the National Assembly decided to censure the prime minister. Dia responded by arresting four of the UPS deputies who had sought to oust him, and Senghor intervened on the side of the deputies. The army resolved the crisis by supporting Senghor and ar-

Figure 2.1. Léopold Sédar Senghor offering advice to Abdou Diouf, his successor. (Photo by Michel Renaudeau)

resting Dia. The prime minister was tried for attempting a coup d'état, found guilty, and sentenced to life imprisonment.

With Dia out of the picture, Senghor moved to change the 1960 constitution to eliminate the office of prime minister and to concentrate greater power in the hands of the president. In a national referendum held on March 3, 1963, the country approved a new constitution that established a strong presidential regime. Senghor and the UPS then prepared for the December 1, 1963, national elections. The unified opposition list included leaders of the Parti du Rassemblement Africain–Sénégal (African Assembly Party of Senegal–PRA-Sénégal), the party that had led the campaign for a no vote in 1958; elements of the Marxist-Leninist Parti Africain de l'Indépendance (African Independence party–PAI), which had been banned in 1960; partisans of Mamadou Dia; and followers of Cheikh Anta Diop, the leader of a faction of the short-lived Dakar-based Bloc des Masses Sénégalaises (Bloc of the Senegalese Masses–BMS), which had refused to rally to the UPS before the elections. The elections themselves were marred by rioting in Dakar and outbreaks of violence in several rural districts. The official election results gave 94.2 percent of the votes to the UPS, a figure that surely exaggerated the party's margin of victory.

The second period[2] (1964–1975) was one in which Senegal was, for all practical purposes, transformed into a one-party state. Throughout this period, the UPS held all seats in the National Assembly and faced no formal political opposition in national or local elections. In October 1964, the government outlawed the Front National Sénégalais (Senegalese National Front–FNS), a coalition of *Diaistes* and supporters of Cheikh Anta Diop. The legal opposition completely disappeared in June 1966 when PRA-Sénégal rallied to the UPS and its leaders–Abdoulaye Ly, Assane Seck, and Moktar M'Bow–were rewarded with ministerial posts and places in the UPS Political Bureau. In the February 28, 1968, national elections the UPS did not have to face any rival political parties.

Despite the absence of opposition parties, the late 1960s was a stormy period for Senghor and the UPS, marked by an attempt to assassinate President Senghor in 1967, student and trade union unrest in the spring of 1968, and general rural discontent popularly known as the *"malaise paysanne."* During this period, Senghor and the UPS managed to survive by making concessions to Senegalese students, workers, and businessmen; co-opting their leaders; and using force when necessary to preserve the regime, as was the case when the army was called upon to crush student and trade union strikes and restore order in May and June 1968.

In 1970 Senghor revised the constitution to restore the office of prime minster and named Abdou Diouf, a young technocrat, to fill it. Senghor and the UPS again ran unopposed in the national elections of January 28, 1973. With the political opposition reduced to impotence, Senghor began to move cautiously to liberalize the regime and to restore the semblance of multiparty democracy.[3] In April 1974 Mamadou Dia and other prominent political prisoners were released to demonstrate the regime's desire for national reconciliation. A few months later, the government formally recognized the Parti Démocratique Sénégalais (Senegalese Democratic party–PDS), led by Abdoulaye Wade, as the country's first legal opposition party since PRA-Sénégal's merger with the

UPS in 1966. In 1975 a presidential pardon permitted Majhemout Diop, the leader of the outlawed PAI, to return to Senegal after fifteen years in exile.

The third period (1976–1980) of the Senghor era was marked by movement toward a competitive multiparty system and preparations for Senghor's departure from the political scene. Revision of the constitution in April 1976 permitted a three-party system in which each of the three competing parties would be identified with one of the "ideological currents" designated in the constitution: social democratic, liberal democratic, and Marxist-Leninist/Communist. The UPS declared that it incarnated the social democratic position, changed its name to Parti Socialiste (Socialist party – PS), and joined the Second Socialist International to demonstrate its commitment to this ideological position. As the government determined which party was to operate under which label, the PDS was obliged to be the liberal democratic party, despite protests by its leaders that it was really closer to Great Britain's Labour party in ideological orientation. Majhemout Diop's resurrected PAI became the officially sanctioned Marxist-Leninist party.

In allowing only three official parties, the 1976 constitutional reforms left opponents of the PS who did not wish to affiliate with either the PDS or the PAI outside the system. Thus, Cheikh Anta Diop's Rassemblement National Démocratique (National Democratic Assembly – RND) was denied formal recognition as a political party, and Mamadou Dia was refused permission to form his own political party. On the other hand, the government permitted Diop, Dia, and other political opponents to publish newspapers that often contained scathing attacks on the Senghor regime.[4]

All three legal political parties competed in the national elections of February 26, 1978, the first presidential and legislative elections to be contested since 1963. The electoral campaign featured mass meetings and televised debates between spokesmen of the contending parties. The PDS and PAI claimed that the state-controlled radio and television stations favored the PS and that local administrative officials were far from neutral in supervising the elections. The official results gave the PS approximately 82 percent of the votes; Abdoulaye Wade and the PDS received nearly 18 percent. The PAI ran a poor third, garnering less than 3,800 of the nearly 1 million votes cast. The percentage of abstentions – slightly more than 37 percent – was the highest since independence, a fact that the opposition attributed to growing popular dissatisfaction with the regime and the "illegal" opposition's call for a boycott of the election. After the election, Mamadou Dia and other opposition leaders claimed that the PS was, in fact, a minority party because a majority of the voters had either abstained or voted against Senghor and the PS.

The Senegalese constitution was again revised in 1979 to make room for a fourth political party to carry the banner of the right. The government formally recognized the Mouvement Républicain Sénégalais (Senegalese Republican Movement—MRS) as the country's fourth legal party in February 1979. The conservative MRS champions private property, free enterprise, and traditional Islamic and African family values; it is headed by Boubacar Guèye, a prominent Dakar lawyer and nephew of Lamine Guèye.

While liberalizing Senegalese politics, Senghor was at the same time setting the stage for his eventual withdrawal from the political scene. Aware of his own mortality, Senghor had carefully planned the succession. Since the office of prime minister had been restored in 1970, Senghor had been grooming Abdou Diouf to be his successor. The Senegalese constitution was revised in April 1976 to permit the prime minister to automatically take over the duties of the president in case the president died or resigned from office and to continue as president until the next presidential election. Senghor also built up Diouf's stature as a national leader by sending him to represent Senegal on important diplomatic missions. By resigning at the end of 1980, Senghor ensured that his successor could remain in office without having to face the electorate until April 1983, when the president's term was scheduled to end.

The coming to power of Abdou Diouf on New Year's Day, 1981, marked the beginning of the post-Senghor era in Senegalese politics. Upon assuming the presidency, Diouf pledged that his regime would continue Senghor's policies. But he also intimated that he would not necessarily govern the country in the same style as his illustrious mentor. In fact, Diouf, during his first year in office, took several bold steps to distinguish his regime from that of his predecessor (see Chapter 6).

THE POLITICAL PROCESS:
CLAN POLITICS AND PARTY STRUCTURES

It would be impossible to comprehend the flavor and essence of Senegalese politics without some understanding of the important role played by "clan politics" in the country's political life.[5] During the postwar era, Senegal's two major political parties were built around coalitions of different groups of leaders and their followers. At the local level, clan politics incorporated large numbers of people into the game of electoral politics and linked the mass of the population to regional and national leaders. When interparty electoral competition declined after independence, clan politics persisted, primarily in the form of intraparty factionalism among rival politicians jockeying for control over local and regional party organizations.

Senegalese clan politics is highly personalized and revolves around the prestige of the clan leader and his ability to reward followers with favors, material resources, and reflected glory. In the context of Senegalese politics, clan leaders are not necessarily professional politicians. They can also be religious leaders, rural notables, heads of ethnic communities, businessmen, or trade unionists vying for power within their own community or organization.

Clan politics was clearly a major ingredient in the 1962 power struggle between Senghor and Mamadou Dia that led to the latter's downfall. While prime minister (1957–1962), Dia took advantage of his control over government jobs and resources to build a large following of local and regional clan leaders. When politicians aligned with Dia seized control of local party organizations previously held by pro-Senghor clan leaders, the latter became alarmed and told Senghor that Dia was planning to replace him as party leader. The UPS became increasingly polarized into two camps, with clan leaders lining up behind either the prime minister or the president. Although Dia attracted a considerable share of local and regional UPS party officials to his banner, he failed in his efforts to win the support of Senegal's most important clan leaders—the marabouts heading the Mouride and Tijani brotherhoods, who remained loyal to Senghor because they were wary of Dia's plans to limit their political influence. Pro-Senghor deputies had a majority in the National Assembly, and it was they who introduced the motion of censure that brought the crisis to a head. With the marabouts and the army on Senghor's side, Dia had no chance of winning even though he had a large number of supporters within the party and government. After ousting Dia, Senghor proceeded to purge the government and the UPS of individuals and clan leaders who had sided with the prime minister.[6]

Although he often denounced the evils of clan politics—"la politique politicienne"—Senghor himself was a master of this style of politics. He knew how to keep on the good side of the dominant factions controlling the Muslim brotherhoods and how to play off rival clan leaders against each other to weaken or win control of trade unions or business organizations. He was particularly adept at squashing potential challengers before they could establish independent power bases within the party. For example, in 1978, when it became clear that Boubacar Ba, the ambitious finance minister and a rising light in the PS, was preparing to contest Senghor's choice for the succession, Senghor intervened to break Ba's hold over the Sine-Saloum regional party organization by throwing his support to the "clan" backing Abdou Diouf. When Ba's followers were defeated by the Diouf clan, Ba himself lost his regional party base, was forced to resign from the government, and went into political oblivion.

The party structures that Abdou Diouf inherited after taking Senghor's place as secretary-general of the PS in January 1981 did not differ very much from those in place at independence. Thus, the PS was organized at all levels of society, from the village and neighborhood committees at the base to the Political Bureau at the national level. During the Senghor era, party congresses were held nearly every year and provided the occasion for Senghor to present to the faithful scholarly lectures that laid down the broad outlines of government policy and exhorted the *militants* (party rank and file) to give up their wicked ways—e.g., clan politics, nepotism, and corruption. The National Council also met three or four times a year to discuss major national issues. In recent years, the councils have centered primarily around such economic issues as national water policy, reforestation, and rural economic reform. Party congresses and national councils also serve to place the official party stamp of approval on government domestic and foreign policies and to reaffirm the party's confidence in the national leader. In Senegal, as in most African states, national policy tends to be made at the top and then filters down to the rank and file at the base.

A mass party, the PS also has its own party youth and women's movements and close ties with labor. The youth movement serves as a training ground for young PS cadres and provides an important base for advancement for ambitious party youth (defined as anyone under 30). During the past few years, Western-educated Senegalese women have been playing a more prominent role within the PS, their enhanced status recognized by the presence of the president of the National Women's Movement on the Political Bureau. The secretary-general of the nation's largest trade union also has a seat on the Political Bureau. The PS has its own official newspaper, *L'Unité Africaine*, which appears monthly, providing party news and countering the attacks of the opposition.

While the top party organs are dominated by the intellectual elite, local party organizations at the grassroots level are more representative of Senegalese society and more concerned with the day-to-day "bread and butter" issues of jobs, services, and government contracts for the faithful. Although prominent rural notables are often involved in party politics, little party activity takes place at the village level. Party organization remains largely an urban phenomenon, taking place in Cap Vert in the form of big-city machine politics or in the small towns in the interior as the affair of local officials and elites. Since the late 1970s, however, there has been a sharp increase in party activities in the rural areas, stimulated by the establishment of elective Rural Councils and the possibility for opposition political parties to run their own candidates for political office in competition with those of the PS.

THE POLITICAL PROCESS: IDEOLOGICAL AND INTEREST-GROUP POLITICS

Unlike clan politics, which is based on patron-client relationships and a share of the spoils of office, ideological politics in Senegal is primarily concerned with winning the hearts and minds of the Western-educated intellectual elite. Until recently, most of Senegal's intellectuals and political parties have affirmed their allegiance to some variant of socialist ideology.

It is difficult to understand Senegalese ideological politics without some appreciation of the influence of the French left on Senegalese intellectuals. This influence reached its peak during the postwar era (1946–1960), when most Senegalese university students attended school in France and many adopted Marxism or Marxism-Leninism as their guiding philosophy.[7] This should not be surprising, as many French university professors were themselves Marxists and the French left, particularly the French Communist party, supported anticolonial independence movements throughout Africa and the Third World. After finishing their studies, former militant student leaders like Majhemout Diop and Abdoulaye Ly returned to Senegal in the late 1950s to agitate for independence and organize the radical Senegalese left.

Meanwhile, Léopold Sédar Senghor and Mamadou Dia were in the process of formulating a non-Marxist socialist ideology that had much in common with the communitarian socialism espoused by Emmanuel Mounier, Catholic philosopher, editor of *Esprit*, and one of the leading lights of the French Catholic left.[8] While recognizing the need for economic planning and the elimination of "man's exploitation of man," Senghor and Dia rejected the Marxist concept of historical materialism and the class struggle as the main motors of human history and stressed the primacy of cooperation over conflict in human relations. Senghor formulated the philosophical and political bases of African Socialism while Mamadou Dia developed its economic components.[9]

When the UPS took power, African Socialism became the official ideology of the regime. Senegalese intellectuals on the Marxist left argued that African Socialism was not a valid socialist ideology but simply a rationale for defending the status quo and the preservation of neocolonial relationships with France. Senghor and Dia insisted that African Socialism was indeed an authentic socialist ideology that made more sense in Senegal than the Marxist ideologies imported from Europe because it was based on African communitarian traditions and values. While he was prime minister, Dia took a more militant socialist stance toward the private sector than Senghor, thus arousing the enmity of the French and Senegalese business communities without winning the support of the Senegalese left opposition.

After Dia's ouster, Senghor, while reaffirming his government's commitment to African Socialism, downplayed socialist rhetoric in his major policy pronouncements. Within the government, the technocratic perspective gained ground over the agrarian socialist perspective of the early 1960s.[10] Despite the rallying of the PRA-Sénégal leadership to the UPS, ideological opposition from the Marxist left continued to be strong throughout the remainder of the decade. The disappearance of opposition political parties and contested national elections deprived the Marxist left of a public forum to express its views, and ideological politics was forced underground.

Ideology again became a major factor in Senegalese politics following the restoration of legal opposition parties and the emergence of a vigorous opposition press during the mid-1970s. At that time, the regime once again utilized ideological appeals to win the support of students and intellectuals in the opposition by reiterating its socialist credentials. Thus, the 1972 Administrative Reform was implemented in the name of African Socialism; the UPS changed its name to Parti Socialiste; and Senghor began a diplomatic offensive to organize an inter-African socialist movement of African parties committed to the principles of democratic socialism.

By the end of the 1970s, the moderate socialist ideology of the PS was once again under sharp attack by several ideological currents on the left and vigorously defended in public debate by Senghor and other PS leaders. The freer political atmosphere of the late 1970s and early 1980s also permitted the generation of other ideological positions, which had been largely absent in the past. Thus, the newly created MRS proclaimed the sacred nature of private property and openly advocated a free enterprise system for Senegal, and some militant Muslim fundamentalists have called for an Islamic republic. Since Diouf's accession to power, references to Islamic values have become an important component of PS ideological statements.

Interest-group politics is another major dimension of the Senegalese political system and takes place at two levels. At one level, different political actors and parties strive to win the support of or capture the organizations of key groups within Senegalese society. At the second level, interest groups attempt to wrest concessions from the government while the government pressures the interest groups to go along with its policies.

During the postwar era, four groups played key roles in Senegalese politics: students, labor, African businessmen, and Muslim leaders. University and high school students were the most radical elements in Senegalese society, and they led the nationalist opposition to colonial rule. Labor consisted of those people working in the modern sectors of the economy who joined trade unions to seek higher wages, better working conditions, and the end of discriminatory employment practices. Like the students, they tended to be more militant and less integrated into the competitive party politics of the day. African businessmen went into politics in the hopes of improving their economic status vis-à-vis the French and Lebanese business communities and played an important role as political organizers in both the towns and in the countryside. Finally, Muslim leaders defended the interests of Senegal's Islamic brotherhoods and delivered the mass support a party needed to win national elections.

Since independence, students have been the most persistent source of opposition and the University of Dakar a hotbed of radical politics. During the early 1960s, Senegalese students tended to find the radical nationalism and Marxism of PRA-Senegal and the PAI more appealing than the moderate African Socialism and pro-French orientation of the UPS. After the elimination of opposition political parties, radical student organizations became the main centers of legal opposition to the regime. In May 1968, university students launched a strike, ostensibly to protest cuts in government support for scholarships. The strike soon spread to the secondary schools. The government responded by arresting the student strike leaders and bringing in the army to expel the students and shut down the university. Once the crisis was resolved, the government moved to meet some of the students' demands for more scholarship money and Africanization of the university. Ironically, university students constitute one of the most privileged groups in Senegalese society, receiving monthly stipends and other benefits that exceed those of many Senegalese industrial workers.

During the Senghor era, the regime sought to neutralize student opposition by establishing UPS/PS–affiliated youth and student groups, co-opting radical student leaders with offers of good positions in the government, giving priority in government spending to secondary and university education over primary education, and accelerating the pace of Africanization of the public sector to provide more employment opportunities for university and secondary school graduates.

After several years of relative tranquility, student unrest flared up again during the late 1970s. In 1980 a strike by angry secondary school students in Ziguinchor spread to Dakar and moved the government to use force to break the strike. In 1981 President Diouf organized a conference to discuss the future of Senegalese education. The government's conciliatory stance and promises to implement reforms advocated by radical student and teacher organizations reduced tensions and defused some of the student opposition to the regime (see Chapter 6).

The collaboration of Senegal's trade unions is essential for maintaining political and social stability. After the 1959 national elections, the Dia government moved quickly to domesticate the trade union movement, first by crushing the radical Union Générale des Travailleurs Sénégalais (General Union of Senegalese Workers – UGTAN) through harsh strike-breaking measures and then by promoting the establishment of a UPS-dominated trade union movement, the Union National des Travailleurs Sénégalais (National Union of Senegalese Workers – UNTS). By the end of 1962 all Senegal's trade unions were unified under the UNTS banner. UNTS had to maintain a delicate balance between defending the interests of its members and supporting the economic programs of the government. The trade union movement went through a major crisis when the UNTS leadership called for a national strike in May 1968 to protest government policies that had frozen wages since 1961 and led to a sharp drop in workers' living standards. The government retaliated by arresting the union leaders instigating the strike, dissolving the UNTS, and backing the establishment of the Conféderation Nationale des Travailleurs Sénégalais (National Confederation of Senegalese Workers – CNTS), founded by Doudou N'Gom, a UPS trade union loyalist. As usual, the Senghor regime used both the carrot and the stick to maintain control. The stick consisted of measures to amend the Labor Code in 1971 to limit the right to strike, the imprisonment of trade union leaders who called for or led illegal strikes, and the recognition of the CNTS as Senegal's only legal trade union. The carrot consisted of efforts to meet some of labor's demands by raising the minimum wage, stepping up the Africanization of the modern sector, and offering trade union leaders official representation in the party and the government.

With the liberalization of Senegalese politics, the government in 1976 again permitted the creation of new trade unions not affiliated with the CNTS. In 1977 two competing teachers' unions emerged, the pro-government Syndicat National des Enseignants du Sénégal (National Union of Senegalese Teachers – SNES) and the Syndicat Unique et Démocrate des Enseignants du Sénégal (Sole Democratic Union of Senegalese Teachers – SUDES), which became a major center of radical opposition to the Senghor regime. And some new trade unions like the Union des Travailleurs Libres du Sénégal (Union of Free Senegalese Workers – UTLS) have affiliated with the PDS. Today the PS and the government can no longer take Senegalese trade unions for granted and must work hard to win the support of labor.

Senegalese businessmen are a third major interest group in Senegalese politics. Their aspirations to replace the French and Lebanese in the peanut trade were frustrated by the rapid expansion of the cooperative movement and government control over the marketing of the peanut crop. The Senegalese government did little to promote the development of a modern Senegalese private sector before 1968. At that time, an important group of Senegalese businessmen created the Union des Groupements Economiques du Sénégal (Union of Senegalese Economic Groups – UNIGES), which bitterly criticized the government's economic policies and French and Lebanese domination of the Senegalese economy. The regime responded to this challenge by setting up a rival organization, the Conseil Fédéral des Groupements Economiques du Sénégal (Federal Council of Senegalese Economic Groups – COFEGES), which claimed to be more realistic in its demands. Under pressure, the government took steps to Africanize certain sectors of the economy and to provide more credit to Senegalese businessmen. The Dakar Chamber of Commerce, which had been directly controlled by the French, was Africanized in 1969. In 1970 UNIGES merged with COFEGES to form the Groupements Economiques du Sénégal (Economic Groups of Senegal – GES), which remains the country's most influential advocate of Senegalese private-sector interests. Like many other Senegalese organizations, the GES is highly politicized and its leadership closely allied with the party in power. Because of their heavy dependence upon the government for contracts and credit, Senegalese businessmen have not yet been able to act as an autonomous power center strong enough to force the government to make major shifts in favor of the Senegalese private sector.

The heads of Senegal's major Islamic brotherhoods constitute the most influential interest group in the country, largely because of their hold over their mass following.[11] Senghor's ability to retain the confidence of the marabouts helped him defeat Mamadou Dia and later discouraged other politicians from challenging his claim to national leadership. In exchange for their support, the marabouts extract various concessions from the government – subsidies for mosque construction, easy access to government loans, jobs for their followers, preferential treatment from state development agencies, and higher prices for their peanut crops. Unlike the urban-based student, labor, and business interest groups that are heavily dependent upon the government financially, the marabouts, thanks to their large landholdings and the contributions of their followers, have an autonomous economic base that gives them greater freedom vis-à-vis the ruling party.

Toward the end of the Senghor era, the Muslim leaders began to put more distance between themselves and the government. This was particularly true of Abdoul Lahat M'Backé, the grand khalife (spiritual head) of the Mourides, who made a point of not owing any debts to the government. The recent resurgence of Islam in Senegal and the growing dissatisfaction of Muslim leaders with what they consider to be the deterioration of traditional Islamic values under the leadership of Senghor and Senegal's Western-educated and secularized urban elite have led the government to place a much greater stress on Islamic values. With Senghor's departure, this trend will continue and probably be intensified (see Chapter 6).

GOVERNMENT INSTITUTIONS

As in most African countries, the presidency in Senegal is the main locus of political power. The 1960 Senegalese constitution provided for a so-called bicephalous, or two-headed, regime that gave broad powers to both the president and the prime minister. The president was the head of state and conducted foreign policy; the prime minister was chief executive and ran the day-to-day affairs of government. This division of labor satisfied neither Senghor, who resented his lack of control over governmental activities, nor Dia, who sought greater recognition as a national leader. This mutual dissatisfaction was one of the major underlying causes of the breakup of the Senghor-Dia tandem in 1962.

The 1963 constitution transferred the functions previously carried out by the prime minister to the president and placed few checks on presidential power. It gave the president the right to exercise "exceptional powers" and declare a state of siege under certain critical circumstances that he alone would determine. Senghor invoked these powers during the May–June 1968 crisis, when student strikes, trade union agitation, and urban rioting shook the foundations of the regime.

In time, it became evident that the extreme concentration of power in Senghor's hands stifled government initiative, as ministers were reluctant to take action before obtaining the personal approval of the president. In 1969 several Senegalese intellectuals and civil servants closely associated with the president began to call for constitutional reforms to increase the responsibility of cabinet ministers and expand opportunities for political participation. With Senghor's approval, these demands were translated into reality with the February 1970 revisions of the 1963 constitution. The office of the prime minister was reestablished and the right of the National Assembly to dismiss the prime minister and his government through a motion of censure was restored.

Although once again giving the prime minister control over the administration, the 1970 constitutional reforms still left the president clearly in command. In effect, the prime minister had to be the "president's man," because it was the president who appointed him in the first place and who had the power to dismiss him. Moreover, the president still exercised direct control over foreign policy, defense, the army, and the appointment of magistrates. The president also retained the power to dismiss the National Assembly and call for national elections.

During Diouf's tenure as prime minister (1970–1980), the influence of the technocrats in government rose dramatically. Diouf himself exemplified the new breed of technocrats. Highly regarded as a competent technician who "knew his dossiers," Diouf had served as Senghor's *directeur de cabinet* (head staff officer), secretary-general of the government, and planning minister before being named prime minister. He had also been a member of the Club Nation et Développement (Club for Development and the Nation), the group of young Senegalese establishment intellectuals[12] who had inspired the 1970 constitutional reforms. With Diouf as prime minister, several club members entered the government and the number of cabinet posts—held primarily by technocrats—expanded from eighteen in 1970 to twenty-seven by the time Diouf assumed the presidency in 1981.

The National Assembly's role as a major national decision-making center diminished considerably after independence. Ironically, the influence of the National Assembly was greatest during the Dia years (1959–1962), when it exercised considerable influence over budgetary matters. With Dia as prime minister, the deputies complained frequently about executive dominance, the inadequate participation of deputies in the planning process, and the stinginess of the government in allocating resources for roads, schools, wells, dispensaries, and other services demanded by their constituents. With the installation of the presidential regime in 1963, the National Assembly saw its influence reduced still further. It could no longer bring down a government, and deputies had fewer opportunities to initiate legislation and less control over the purse strings. Moreover, strict party discipline and the absence of deputies from opposition parties meant that parliamentary debate was muted and the ratification of government-initiated legislation more or less automatic.

After 1978 the National Assembly again became a lively forum for debating the major political and economic issues confronting the country. Abdoulaye Wade's PDS won 18 seats in the February 1978 national elections, and although it is unable to affect legislation, it has used its forum in the National Assembly to attack the PS government's policies and gain a wider public hearing.

Senegal's judicial branch of government[13] is headed by a Supreme Court, which is the last court of appeal and rules on the constitutionality of government laws, regulations, and actions. In principle, the independence of the judiciary is guaranteed by the constitution.

Magistrates cannot be removed from office without their consent, and in carrying out their duties they are not to be pressured by representatives of the executive or legislative branches of government. In practice, however, the courts have rarely ruled against the government in important constitutional cases or political trials, a fact that should not be surprising, as the magistrates are named by the president.

Senegalese clearly have the right to their day in court when they wish to contest the legality of government actions. Since the liberalization of Senegalese political life in the mid-1970s, the courts have become a major battleground of Senegalese politics. When the Senghor government revised the constitution in 1974 to permit a limited number of political parties representing defined ideological currents to operate legally, the RND, led by Cheikh Anta Diop, challenged the constitutionality of the measure and took its case to the Supreme Court after the government refused to let the RND register as a legal party. Diop and the RND argued that the government had no right to define the ideological stance that a political party must take or to restrict the number of parties. In January 1978, the Supreme Court threw out the RND's case on a technicality by ruling that its request for official recognition had been filed too late. Although the RND lost that battle, it eventually won its point when the Senegalese National Assembly lifted restrictions on the number of political parties in April 1981.

High-ranking government officials and other establishment figures have gone to the courts to protect themselves against allegedly scurrilous attacks and libelous charges published in the opposition press. During the late 1970s and early 1980s, the head of the Senegalese National Development Bank, a leading Senegalese army general, the editor of *Le Soleil*, the progovernment daily, and Abdou Diouf all sued various newspapers for defamation of character and called upon the state to prosecute the accused journalist. In most instances, the aggrieved parties won their cases, with the result being fines, temporary suspension of the offending newspapers, and sometimes short prison terms for the guilty journalists. The opposition protested that such actions violated the freedom of the press and were used to silence criticism of the regime; the government argued that strong measures had to be taken to protect individuals against character assassination and the regime against false charges.

The 1963 constitution set up the Economic and Social Council as an advisory body to the government on economic and social questions. It was established primarily to give representatives of the diverse sectors of the Senegalese economy a voice in formulating national economic policy and to reassure the private sector, which had felt menaced by the Dia government's socialist policies, that it would have a prominent role in Senegal's economic future. Although government employees, workers, farmers, artisans, merchants, industrialists, and experts designated by the government are all represented on it, the Economic and Social Council has tended to reflect the views of the Senegalese and French business communities.

Since its inception, the council has been primarily an organ in the service of the presidency. Senghor used it as an important source of information and analysis when promoting new policies, as an official outlet for recognizing various national and foreign economic interest groups, and as a conduit for dispensing honorific titles for party leaders not serving in the government or the National Assembly.

Although not a formal governmental organ like the National Assembly or the Economic and Social Council, the Senegalese army stands out as one of the nation's major institutions. Since intervening on Senghor's behalf in 1962, the army has been one of the main pillars of the regime, singled out for special recognition and praise as a symbol of national unity during Senegal's annual Independence Day celebrations. Over the years, the Senegalese army has demonstrated its firm commitment to civilian rule and loyalty to the regime in power. In 1980 and 1981, it turned a deaf ear to appeals by various opposition elements to overthrow the government or to intervene more directly in Senegalese politics to ensure fair elections.

During the late 1960s, the army was charged primarily with maintaining internal order and protecting Senegal's southern borders in the Casamance against incursions by Portuguese troops from Guinea-Bissau. After the departure of a large contingent of French troops from Senegal in 1974, the army was modernized and expanded in line with the greater role it was to play as an instrument of Senegalese foreign policy. During the late 1970s, Senegalese troops were sent to Lebanon as part of the UN peacekeeping mission and to Zaire to shore up the Mobutu regime in Shaba Province. Between 1976 and 1980, the size of Senegal's military increased from 5,950 to 10,000. At the Independence Day celebrations on April 4, 1980, Senghor announced that the armed forces' budget would be increased significantly and that the size of the military would rise to 15,000 during the early 1980s because of the threat of external aggression against Senegal and her francophone African allies.[14] After assuming the presidency in 1981, Abdou Diouf pledged to continue the build-up of Senegal's military forces.

POSTCOLONIAL ADMINISTRATIVE REFORMS AND LOCAL GOVERNMENT

Those who took power at independence gained control of the administrative structures, legal system, and police powers of the French colonial state. Reformers rather than revolutionaries, Senegal's national leaders did not wish to dismantle the state structures they had inherited. Instead, they sought to Africanize them and to make the postcolonial state an instrument for promoting national rather than metropolitan goals and priorities. This task required some modification of the inherited colonial administrative structures and the creation of new ones.

The first major reform took place in January 1960 when the Dia government reorganized Senegal's field administration and redrew administrative districts to bring the postcolonial state closer to the rural population. As a result the country was divided into seven *régions*,[15] twenty-eight *cercles*, and eighty-five *arrondissements*, which replaced the thirteen *cercles*, twenty-seven *subdivisions*, and 135 *cantons* established under colonial rule. At this time, the government abolished the unpopular *chefferies* and Africanized all echelons of the territorial administration by replacing the remaining French officials with Senegalese. Subsequent changes in official nomenclature sought to eliminate all vestiges of colonial rule and reaffirm the national identity of the Senegalese administration. Thus in 1964 the *cercle* became the *département* and the old colonial title of *commandant* was replaced by that of *préfet*.

In addition to restructuring the territorial field administration, the 1960 administrative reforms also provided for the creation of new representative institutions in the countryside to democratize Senegalese politics. Thus, the elevation of all departmental capitals to the status of full communes made it possible for the people in Senegal's smaller towns in the interior to elect their own mayors and municipal councils. At the same time, the Dia government established regional assemblies to represent the rural populations living in Senegal's 13,000 villages. Urban dwellers were not eligible to vote, and Cap Vert did not have its own regional assembly because it was a predominantly urban area.

These new institutions became highly politicized and the major battleground of local clan politics. Control over jobs, honorific offices, and communal resources became the spoils of victory for successful party leaders at the local level and the main source of intraparty squabbling. And contrary to the government's original intentions, urban-based UPS politicians and powerful rural notables rather than representatives of grassroots rural communities determined the composition of the regional assemblies.

After the political demise of Mamadou Dia, Senghor took steps to reinforce the central government's control over local government institutions.[16] First, alarmed by the intense and often violent factional intraparty strife touched off by the battle for control over communal resources, Senghor moved to depoliticize local government by tightening

Figure 2.2. Going to the polls. Senegal has one of Black Africa's rare multiparty democracies. (Photo by Michel Renaudeau)

the Interior Ministry's tutelage over the administration of communal budgets, which now had to be approved by the Interior Minister before being executed. Second, Senghor drastically reduced the flow of resources from the central government to the communes to prevent the waste of scarce national resources on expensive city halls, race tracks, and other nonproductive investments and to lower the stakes of local politics. Third, Senghor strengthened the powers of the regional governors and expanded the scope of the territorial administration, while the regional assemblies survived as little more than rubber stamps for approving government-initiated programs. The subordination of local government to administrative control coupled with the elimination of opposition political parties marked a sharp setback to the democratization of Senegalese politics that was not reversed until the mid-1970s.

The Administrative Reform of July 1972 that abolished the regional assemblies and provided for the establishment of the rural community (communauté rurale) as the basic unit of government in the countryside set the stage for greater popular participation in local government. The philosophical underpinning of the reform derived from the ideology of African Socialism articulated by Mamadou Dia and Senghor during the late 1950s and early 1960s. The rural communities, or rural communes, as they were originally called, were conceived as the core political units within a decentralized agrarian socialist society.

The 1972 Administrative Reform called for the establisment of three to four rural communities in each arrondissement. Each rural community had a rural council that was granted broad powers to regulate local markets, fairs, cattle walks, and residential zoning patterns. To prevent domination by rural notables and ensure greater popular participation, village chiefs, cooperative presidents, and those with nonrural occupations were formally excluded from holding the office of president. Each rural council had its own small budget—approximately $40 to $50 thousand—which could be used to finance local community development projects. Councils had the power to allocate uncultivated land and to revise existing land tenure systems in the areas under their jurisdiction.

The 1972 Administrative Reform was first put into effect in the regions of Thiès and Sine-Saloum in 1974, Diourbel and Louga in 1976, the Casamance in 1978, and the Fleuve in 1980. Senegal now has 284 rural communities that encompass the rural population of every interior region but Eastern Senegal, where the reform is scheduled to be implemented in 1982. By mid-1982, the full potential for popular participation had not been realized. In most instances, the central government continued to control the rural communities through the sous-préfet (subprefect), whose presence at rural council meetings intimidated council members and made it more difficult to approve projects and policies not endorsed by the government. Despite the paternalism of the Senegalese administrative officials who oversee the rural councils, the rural communities seemed to be well on their way to becoming a new force in the countryside.

NOTES

1. For a full account of this period, see Sheldon Gellar, "Politics of Development in Senegal," Ph.D. dissertation, Columbia University, 1967, pp. 352–366.

2. For a detailed analysis of the evolution of Senegalese political party and government structures during this period, see Edward J. Schumacher, *Politics, Bureaucracy, and Rural Development in Senegal* (Berkeley: University of California Press, 1975), pp. 25–83.

3. For a scholarly discussion of Senegal's multiparty system, see Ibrahima Fall, *Sous-développement et démocratie multipartisane, L'experience sénégalaise* [Underdevelopment and multiparty democracy, the Senegalese experience] (Dakar: Nouvelles Editions Africaines, 1977). For a perceptive analysis of trends during the early liberalization period, see Donal B. Cruise O'Brien, "Senegal," in John Dunn, ed., *West African States: Failure and Promise* (Cambridge: Cambridge University Press, 1978), pp. 173–188.

4. Senegal now has a wide variety of opposition newspapers, including *Le Démocrate* (PDS), *Momsarev* (PAI), *Taxaw* (RND), *Andë Sopi* (Diaist), *Jaay Doole Bi* (Maoist), and *Verité* (Marxist-Leninist). Senegal has several other political newspapers not officially aligned with a party or ideological position—*Le Politicien, Promotion,* and *Dieuf Action*—which have also been critical of the regime. The most popular and witty of the three is *Le Politicien,* which is a Senegalese version of France's satirical *Le Canard Enchaîné.* The most widely read paper—Senegal's only daily newspaper—is the progovernment *Le Soleil,* formerly known as *Dakar-Matin* until its Africanization in 1970.

5. For excellent discussions of clan politics and political factionalism in Senegal, see Jonathan S. Barker, "Political Factionalism in Senegal," *Canadian Journal of African Studies* 7, 2 (1973):287–303; William J. Foltz, "Social Structure and Political Behavior of Senegalese Elites," *Behavior Science Notes* 4, 2 (1969):145–163; and Donal B. Cruise O'Brien, *Saints and Politicians: Essays in the Organization of a Senegalese Peasant Society* (Cambridge: Cambridge University Press, 1975), pp. 149–182.

6. For a detailed analysis of UPS party structures see François Zuccarelli, *Un parti politique africaine: L'Union Progressiste Sénégalaise* [An African political party: The Senegalese Progressive Union] (Paris: R. Pichon and R. Durand-Auzias, 1970).

7. See Jean-Pierre N'Diaye's *Enquête sur les étudiants noires en France* [A survey of Black African students in France] (Paris: Editions Réalités Africaines, 1962) for an extensive survey of francophone African student opinions during this crucial formative period.

8. See Sheldon Gellar, Robert B. Charlick, and Yvonne Jones, *Animation Rurale and Rural Development: The Experience of Senegal* (Ithaca, N.Y.: Cornell University Rural Development Committee, 1980), pp. 34–47, for a discussion of the influence of the Catholic left on Senegalese African Socialist ideology.

9. See Léopold Sédar Senghor, *On African Socialism* (New York: Frederick A. Praeger, 1964); and Mamadou Dia, *The African Nations and World Solidarity* (New York: Frederick A. Praeger, 1961) for two major examples of their approach.

10. Schumacher, *Politics, Bureaucracy, and Rural Development in Senegal*, pp. 213–218; and Gellar, Charlick, and Jones, *Animation Rurale and Rural Development*, pp. 74–92.

11. See Lucy C. Behrman, *Muslim Brotherhoods and Politics in Senegal* (Cambridge, Mass.: Harvard University Press, 1970); Donal B. Cruise O'Brien, *The Mourides of Senegal: The Political and Economic Organization of an Islamic Brotherhood* (London: Oxford University Press, 1971); and Cheikh Tidiane Sy, *La confrérie sénégalaise des Mourides* [The Senegalese Mouride brotherhood] (Paris: Présence Africaine, 1969).

12. For representative articles reflecting their thinking, see their *Club Nation et Développement* [Club for Development and the Nation] (Paris: Présence Africaine, 1972).

13. For a major study of Senegal's judicial and other governmental institutions, see Jean-Claude Gautron and Michel Rougevin-Baville, *Droit public du Sénégal* [Senegalese public law] (Paris: Editions A. Pedone, 1970).

14. *Marchés Tropicaux*, April 11, 1980, p. 864.

15. The number of regions was expanded to eight when Louga became Senegal's eighth region in 1976.

16. See Clement Cottingham, "Political Consolidation and Centre-Local Relations in Senegal," *Canadian Journal of African Studies* 4, 1 (Winter 1970):101–120.

3

The Economy

At independence, Senegal's national leaders had high hopes for the country's economic future. Through intelligent national planning, they believed, Senegal could accelerate its rate of economic growth, narrow the economic gap between Dakar and the countryside, diversify the economy, and reduce dependency. These hopes remain largely unfulfilled after more than two decades of independence. At the beginning of the 1980s, real per capita incomes had actually declined; the economy still revolved around the peanut; and the country was in some ways even more dependent upon external economic forces than before.

Senegal's uphill battle to promote national economic development has faced enormous obstacles. Constraints imposed by the structural underdevelopment and patterns of dependency inherited from the colonial period have severely limited Senegal's economic options. Chronic drought conditions have canceled out short-term gains in agriculture. As an energy-poor country, Senegal has been particularly hard hit by rapidly rising oil prices and deteriorating terms of trade that have raised its annual trade deficits to almost catastrophic proportions. Finally, Senegal's current difficulties have been aggravated by a bloated state bureaucracy and widespread corruption in several key government agencies.

Senegal's economic problems are by no means atypical. On the contrary, they reveal how difficult it is for resource-poor, low-income Third World countries like Senegal to escape the trap of underdevelopment and dependence. Yet Senegal's situation is not hopeless. Although its economic prospects for the next few years are bleak, its long-run prospects are much better and offer some hope for the future.

SENEGALESE ECONOMIC STRUCTURES: SAHELIAN AND MARITIME SENEGAL

Senegal's annual per capita income is approximately $350–$400.[1] This aggregate figure tells us little, however, about the great disparities in income and economic structures between Sahelian and Maritime

45

Senegal. In Sahelian Senegal, the rural masses struggle for survival; in Maritime Senegal, the urban masses battle for a better position within a relatively modern economy.

In Sahelian Senegal, agriculture is based largely upon the cultivation of peanuts, millet, and sorghum, crops that grow quickly and require relatively little rainfall. Most rural Senegalese live in areas where rainfall is sparse and irregular and drought a common occurrence. Herders and farmers in the north of the country, where the average rainfall varies between 10 and 20 inches (250 and 500 mm) a year are the most vulnerable to drought. The situation is somewhat better in central Senegal, which encompasses the country's main peanut-producing areas, where rainfall averages between 20 and 30 inches (500 and 800 mm) a year. But even in rice-producing regions like the Lower Casamance, where annual rainfall averages more than 40 inches (1,000 mm) a year, subnormal rainfall can be a serious problem, because rice requires more water than peanuts or millet.

Sahelian Senegal's rural economy[2] is based primarily on the peanut, which takes up more than 40 percent of the land under cultivation. Agricultural productivity in Sahelian Senegal is low. Its agriculture does not produce sufficient food to adequately feed Senegal's rural populations, let alone generate a surplus large enough to feed the country's rapidly growing urban population. Population pressures on the land, shorter fallow periods, and soil erosion have reduced soil productivity in the densely populated areas of western Senegal (60–100 people per square kilometer) that were the first to cultivate peanuts as a cash crop. Except for the more recently settled pioneer zones south and east of Kaolack, where land is more plentiful, landholdings have become increasingly fragmented. Even though many of Senegal's most prominent Muslim leaders own large estates, the marabouts control less than 1 percent of Senegal's farmlands. Sahelian Senegal is made up primarily of small family farms exploited chiefly by family labor. More than two-thirds of the country's farms are less than 10 acres (4 hectares) in size; only 5 percent are more than 25 acres (10 hectares).

Like most Sahelian countries, Senegal has an important livestock sector. However, only a tiny fraction of Senegal's 2–2.5 million cattle are marketed on a commercial scale. Drought periodically decimates Senegal's cattle herds. The country lost 365,000 cattle during the great droughts of the early 1970s and a similar number in 1980, when drought struck again. Despite the significance of cattle as a source of wealth and security, the average Sahelian Senegalese family relies more on goats and sheep for sustenance and supplementary income in hard times.

Life in Sahelian Senegal is difficult. Infant mortality is high; one of five babies does not survive its first year. Malaria and other endemic

Figure 3.1. The great drought of 1973: Starving cattle roam the countryside in search of food. (Photo by United Nations/AID, R. B. Purcell)

diseases afflict most of the rural population. Few villages have safe water supplies, and polluted water sources make it difficult to check the spread of disease. The villages of Sahelian Senegal are not electrified. Firewood remains the principal source of energy, a source that has been dwindling because of deforestation. Life is particularly hard for women, who must spend many hours each day gathering firewood, drawing water, and pounding grain simply to meet minimal family needs.

The dynamism and relatively high income levels of Maritime Senegal, which encompasses all of the Cap Vert peninsula and much of the coastal band between Thiès and Saint Louis, contrast markedly with the poverty of Sahelian Senegal. Maritime Senegal has one of West Africa's best natural deepwater ports, plentiful fishing resources, phosphates, and an attractive climate. It contains most of the country's modern industries, banking and financial institutions, luxury hotels, and a major international trade center. Its population is growing two to three times faster than that of Sahelian Senegal, where the annual rate of increase is estimated to be 2.2 percent.

Living conditions and economic opportunities are generally much better in Maritime Senegal. Per capita income in Cap Vert, for example, is close to $1000, several times the $75–150 per capita incomes of rural Senegal. Those living in Maritime Senegal have better access to doctors, pharmacies, hospitals, and maternity clinics. Most of their children attend public school and eat better than their cousins in the countryside. Thanks to more reliable drinking water supplies, there is less suffering from some of the endemic diseases prevalent in Sahelian Senegal. Maritime Senegal draws large numbers of young people from the interior seeking better educational and employment opportunities. During the dry season (November to May), it also attracts thousands of seasonal workers seeking to supplement low rural incomes.

Class structures are more complex[3] and disparities in living standards are greater within Maritime Senegal than in Sahelian Senegal. Despite the relative prosperity of the region and the presence of an expanding Senegalese "middle" class making up 20–25 percent of the population, the majority of people living in Maritime Senegal are poor and must struggle to make ends meet. Dakar has its sprawling slums and shantytowns, and its unemployment rate may be as high as 25–50 percent in the modern wage sector.

SENEGALESE ECONOMIC STRUCTURES: PEANUT MONOCULTURE AND DIVERSIFICATION

After more than two decades of independence, Senegal's economic health is still closely tied to the vicissitudes of the peanut monoculture economy inherited from the colonial era. The size of the peanut crop is the most important factor affecting the economy; it touches all sectors of the economy. Peanuts generate from two-thirds to three-fourths of the rural population's monetary income, provide the raw materials for Senegal's peanut-processing industries, and constitute the country's leading export product. Since 1960, peanut production has fluctuated between 400,000 and 1,400,000 metric tons a year.[4] A poor crop – say, less than 600,000 metric tons – deals a hard blow to the economy. The peasants suffer from reduced purchasing power; business slackens; the peanut oil industry operates well below capacity; Senegal's light consumer-goods industries reduce their output; urban unemployment rises; trade deficits worsen; the state loses a good deal of revenue; and the gross domestic product drops even when there are significant gains in other sectors of the economy. On the other hand, a good peanut crop – say, more than 1 million tons – stimulates economic recovery and expansion. Then rural purchasing power rises; the peanut oil industry runs at full capacity; commerce picks up; exports climb again; and the state increases its revenues.

Although diversification of the rural economy has been touted as a major objective of national economic policy since the early days of independence, the government did little to introduce new cash crops until

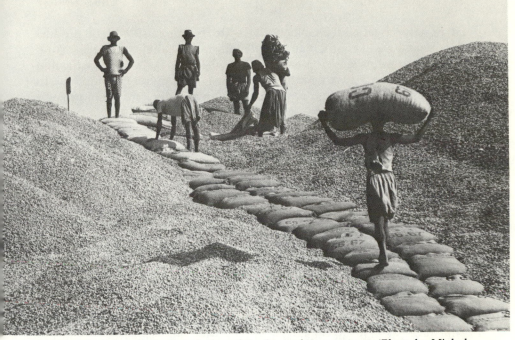

Figure 3.2. Peanuts, the foundation of the Senegalese economy. (Photo by Michel Renaudeau)

the late 1960s and early 1970s, when it began to promote cotton production in Eastern Senegal and the Upper Casamance and sugarcane and tomatoes in the Senegal River delta. Up to that time, government agricultural policy was concerned primarily with raising peanut production and productivity in the peanut basin.

During the mid-1970s, the government began to shift its emphasis to food production. In 1977 it initiated a food investment strategy designed to increase millet production in the peanut basin and rice production in the Fleuve and the Casamance. Official millet prices were raised by 25 percent in 1978, to nearly the level offered for peanuts. The farmers responded to these new incentives by devoting more land and effort to millet. The 1978-1979 millet crop topped 800,000 tons, and for the first time since independence, Senegalese farmers sold their surplus millet in large quantities through official government channels. Senegal's main hope of attaining food self-reliance, however, lies with irrigated rice production. An estimated 250,000 hectares can be brought into irrigated production in the future, including 200,000 hectares in the Senegal River basin and 50,000 hectares in the Casamance. These are optimistic projections and depend largely on Senegal's obtaining massive foreign aid to finance irrigation schemes and on the willingness of Senegalese farmers to abandon traditional agricultural techniques and adopt new irrigation technologies. Despite the emphasis on food production, peanuts will continue to be the mainstay of Sahelian Senegal's rural economy until at least the early 1990s when Senegal's major irrigation schemes for the Fleuve and the Casamance become fully operational. In the meantime, Senegalese economic growth and diversification projects will remain concentrated in Maritime Senegal.

Although the peanut has retained its dominant position within the Senegalese economy, its relative importance has declined since independence. During the early 1960s, peanut products accounted for more than two-thirds of the value of Senegalese exports; by the end of the 1970s, this figure had dropped to 40 percent. Poor peanut crops and low peanut prices, coupled with the growth of other economic sectors – e.g., phosphates, fishing, and tourism – have contributed to the decline in the importance of the peanut. During the late 1950s, Senegal was just beginning to exploit its phosphate resources at Taiba. Today, Senegal is the world's seventh-largest producer of phosphates, mining and marketing more than 1.5 million tons a year. Senegal's maritime fishing industry has nearly quadrupled its production since 1960, and Senegalese fish products have become the country's third major export after peanuts and phosphates. Tourism grew spectacularly during the middle and late 1970s. Industrial output has also risen steadily, averaging 4–5 percent a year despite the ups and downs of the peanut oil industry, whose output rises and falls according to the size of the previous year's peanut crop. Senegal produces a wide range of manufactured goods – e.g., textiles, shoes, petrochemical products, cement, soft drinks, and beer – and exports part of its industrial production to other African nations. Over the years, there has thus been a shift away from the peanut monoculture economy inherited from the colonial era toward a more modern and semi-industrialized economy. This process has been held back by the stagnation of the agricultural sector, which remains the Achilles' heel of the Senegalese economy.

A DEPENDENT ECONOMY

Senegal provides a classic example of a dependent economy whose economic growth and prosperity are largely conditioned by external economic forces and actors. Senegalese economic dependency under colonialism was directed toward France. The metropole determined Senegal's economic policies and pattern of development while Frenchmen controlled the leading sectors of the colonial economy. Like most colonial powers, France also discouraged nonmetropolitan investments in Senegal and oriented Senegal's foreign trade toward France and the franc zone.

A few simple statistics will suffice to illustrate the Senegalese economy's extreme dependency upon France at independence: (1) Approximately 80 percent of Senegal's foreign trade was with France; (2) Nearly all Senegal's peanut exports during the late 1950s and early 1960s were bought by France at subsidized prices 15 to 20 percent above the world market price; (3) France supplied two-thirds of Senegal's public development capital and nearly all of the foreign technical and financial assistance; (4) French investors provided more than 90 percent of the private capital and owned most of the enterprises in the capital-intensive sectors of the Senegalese economy; and (5) the French treasury covered Senegal's foreign trade deficits.

The first decade of independence brought few major changes in the old colonial patterns of dependency.[6] Peanuts continued to provide the bulk of Senegalese exports, and France retained its dominant position as Senegal's major trade and aid partner. During this period of "neocolonial" dependency, France's European Economic Community (EEC) partners developed closer ties with Senegal and other francophone Black African countries. The old colonial tariff structures favoring French goods were modified to give non-French EEC nations equal access to Senegalese markets, and the European Development Fund (EDF) provided Senegal with a new source of multilateral aid. However, the economic aid received from the EEC did not compensate for the 20 percent drop in the value of Senegalese peanut exports when the French stopped buying Senegalese peanuts at subsidized prices in 1967. The end of the subsidy and depressed world market prices for peanuts led to a marked deterioration of the terms of trade between Senegalese exports and imports, which aggravated Senegal's already chronic trade deficits.

The first half of the 1970s was a transition period in which drought and rapidly changing world market conditions moved Senegal to take steps to break out of the old colonial patterns of dependency upon France and the peanut. In 1973 worldwide food shortages and the Arab oil embargo sparked by the Yom Kippur War drove up the price of food imports, led to a fourfold increase in oil prices, and set off a wave of inflation that had a tremendously destabilizing effect on the Senegalese economy. The 1972-1973 drought sharply reduced Senegalese peanut exports, increased food imports, and led to record trade deficits. Shortly afterward, however, dramatic increases in the world market prices of peanuts and phosphates gave the Senegalese some hope for the future as the value of phosphate exports soared from 5.7 billion francs CFA in 1973 to 27.5 billion francs CFA in 1974 and the value of Senegalese peanut exports more than doubled to 34 billion francs CFA despite a mediocre peanut crop. In 1975, the Senegalese government became a majority shareholder in the country's phosphate mining companies and established a state-controlled corporation charged with handling all Senegalese peanut exports. The government counted upon the profits generated by high peanut and phosphate prices to finance several large-scale projects designed to diversify the economy and reduce Senegal's great dependency upon the peanut. At the same time, the government borrowed heavily in international private capital markets at relatively high interest rates on the assumption that world peanut and phosphate prices would not go down, thus allowing Senegal to keep its foreign debt at a manageable level.

After a brief period of favorable world market conditions during the mid-1970s, peanut and phosphate prices dropped sharply, thus depriving Senegal of the revenues needed to repay its loans and finance its major development projects. Senegal's financial difficulties were further aggravated by the return of drought to Senegal during the late 1970s and another round of OPEC-inspired steep increases in oil prices. This combination brought the Senegalese economy to the brink of bankruptcy by the end of the 1970s.

At the beginning of the 1980s, the Senegalese economy was more than ever hostage to external economic forces. Dependency upon the peanut and upon France as Senegal's dominant trade partner had diminished somewhat since independence, but new forms of dependency had emerged. During the 1960s, oil imports had accounted for no more than 5 percent of Senegal's total import bill. In 1970, the oil bill was only 2.5 billion francs CFA; in 1980 it was 50 billion francs CFA, or nearly half the total value of Senegal's exports that year. Rapid urban growth and periodic drought had also steadily increased the demand for food imports, especially for grain imports – e.g., rice, wheat, and millet – which averaged more than 20 billion francs CFA annually. Finally, Senegal's foreign debt was no longer a simple matter that could be resolved by transfers from the French treasury, as had been the case during the neocolonial 1960s. By the end of the 1970s Senegal's foreign debt had climbed to well over $1 billion, and its debt servicing had jumped from a manageable 5–6 percent of exports during the mid-1970s to more than 20 percent by the end of the decade. In 1979, the Senegalese government met with representatives of the International Monetary Fund (IMF) to ask for standby credit to refinance its foreign debt. In December 1979 Prime Minister Diouf announced a new IMF-inspired five-year (1980–1985) economic recovery program (*plan de redressement*) designed to cut government spending, promote economic growth, and reduce Senegal's trade deficits and foreign debt.

One bright note in an otherwise grim situation was Senegal's ability to attract large volumes of foreign aid from the West and from Muslim oil-producing countries to keep the sinking economy afloat. Since 1975,

Senegal has received more than $1 billion in aid, which has permitted the country to feed its people and initiate several large-scale development programs. But with the increased volume of aid has come greater economic dependency. Senegal now relies upon foreign grants and loans to finance 85–90 percent of its new development projects. In the next few years, Senegal will need even larger amounts of aid to refinance its foreign debt and to provide sufficient capital for the dam construction and irrigation schemes that the government sees as the best instrument for escaping from the dependency trap.

AFRICANIZATION AND NATIONALIZATION

During the first decade of independence, Africanization of the Senegalese economy proceeded very slowly. The main priority of the Dia government was to gain control over the peanut trade.[7] In 1960 the government established a state-controlled Senegalese development bank (Banque Sénégalaise de Développement – BSD)[8] and an agricultural marketing board (Office de Commercialisation Agricole – OCA) to break the hold of the French banks and trading companies over the financing of the peanut *traite*. The BSD extended credit to the OCA, which in turn extended credit to the state-sponsored peanut marketing cooperatives. Producers not organized into cooperatives had to sell their peanuts to collecting stations run by private entrepreneurs licensed by the OCA. During the OCA's first year of operations (1960–1961), licensed African purchasing agents still received most of their credit from European trading companies and peanut oil firms. However in 1961, with creation of the Union Sénégalaise de Banque (USB), a commercial bank in which the state held the majority of shares, the OCA also assumed control over credit extended to private companies involved in the peanut trade. This gave the state total control over the financial circuits of the domestic peanut trade and accelerated the withdrawal of the large French trading companies from the interior. The "nationalization" of the peanut trade did little to promote the African private sector, as the state rather than African businessmen replaced the European trading companies as the main economic force in the countryside.

Even though the Dia government took no steps to nationalize other sectors of the economy, the French business community felt uneasy about Dia's plans for the future because of his nationalist sentiments and commitment to socialism. The French welcomed Dia's departure and expressed their full confidence in Senghor, whom they believed would be more conciliatory toward the French. Their expectations were not disappointed. Throughout the rest of the 1960s, Senghor firmly resisted pressures to nationalize other sectors of the Senegalese economy or to accelerate the pace of Africanization in the private sector. Senghor insisted that Senegal did not yet have the capital or technical expertise to undertake large-scale nationalizations and maintained that such measures would frighten potential foreign investors whose capital was needed to industrialize the country. Senghor worked very closely with the French business community, often calling upon Henri-Charles Gallenca, the French president of the Dakar Chamber of Commerce, for economic advice. French industrialists also benefited from the tariff barriers put up by the Senegalese government to protect local French-owned industries against "foreign" competition. Little effort was made to attract non-French foreign capital or to encourage the expansion of the African private sector.

The May–June 1968 crisis reflected widespread dissatisfaction with the slow pace of Africanization and the fact that after nearly a decade of independence, the French, and to a lesser extent the Lebanese, continued to control the leading sectors of the modern economy and to prosper while most Senegalese were suffering from declining living standards.[9] Senegalese trade unions demanded the immediate nationalization of the French-owned water and electricity companies and rapid Africanization of positions still held by skilled European workers and lower- and middle-management employees. African businessmen demanded that certain sectors of the economy, particularly those dominated by the Lebanese, be reserved exclusively for Senegalese Africans and that the government make a greater effort to support the development of the African private sector. The younger generation of Senegalese cadres was also demanding that the government reduce the number of French technical assistance personnel and press the expatriate business community to hire and train more Senegalese for managerial positions.

Senghor responded to these pressures by stepping up the pace of Africanization. In 1969 the government established the Société Nationale d'Etudes et de Promotion Industrielle (National Corporation for the Study and Promotion of Industry – SONEPI) to provide studies, credit, and training to assist the development of small and medium-sized Senegalese firms, and SONEPI became a tangible sign of the government's commitment to promote a Senegalese business class capable of running the modern sectors of the economy.[10] That same year, Senegalese businessmen assumed control over the Dakar Chamber of Commerce and named a Senegalese to replace Gallenca as president. Foreign firms were also pressed to Africanize their personnel and asked to submit plans for "Senegalization." Africanization of personnel was particularly evident in jobs previously held by the French working-class *petits blancs* who had flocked to Senegal during the post–World War II economic boom. By the end of the 1970s nearly all the French skilled workers, mechanics, foremen, and sales clerks had been replaced by Senegalese, and even Lebanese shopkeepers who traditionally relied on family labor had been obliged to hire some Africans.

Africanization of managerial positions progressed much more slowly. By the mid-1970s, foreigners still held nearly half the executive positions and 9 percent of middle-management positions.[11] By the end of the decade, however, the traditional preference of French firms for hiring French nationals was declining, partly because of government pressures to Africanize, but also because an expatriate manager cost the company three to five times as much as a Senegalese holding the same job. Many Senegalese cadres now prefer to work for expatriate firms rather than go into government service because salaries in the private sector are much higher than those in government and careers less dependent upon political criteria and connections. Africanization, ironically, is thus making it increasingly difficult for the government to attract Senegal's most highly qualified cadres.

During the early and mid-1970s, the government under the direction of the young and more nationalistic technocrats launched a drive to nationalize important sectors of the Senegalese economy. First the water and electric utilities, which to many Senegalese had become glaring symbols of French neocolonial domination in the 1960s, were nationalized. Then the government moved to exercise direct control over other key sectors of the economy by becoming the majority shareholder in the companies dominating those sectors. Thus, the state bought 50 percent of the shares in the mining companies that produced Senegalese phosphates and created the Société Nationale de Commercialisation des Oléaginaux du Sénégal (SONOCOS), to gain full control over the marketing of Senegalese peanut oil and oilcake exports. This wave of nationalizations took place at a time when world market prices for phosphates and peanuts were at their height.

While the government was nationalizing key sectors of the economy, it was also taking steps to expand the number of parastatal agencies in the country.[12] Between 1970 and 1975, seventy new parastatal companies were created, primarily to stimulate investments in sectors neglected by private capital. Many of these parastatal companies were set up to attract foreign investors to work in partnership with the government to develop industry, mining, and tourism. For example, the government established a company (SOPRIZI – Société d'aménagement et de Promotion de la zone franche industrielle de Dakar) to promote a tax-free industrial zone in the port of Dakar to draw foreign capital to export-oriented industries. And in 1975, another company (MIFERSO – Mines de Fer du Sénégal Oriental) was created with the participation of French, German, and Japanese capital to explore the possibilities of exploiting Eastern Senegal's iron ore reserves. Several mixed companies were also set up to promote the development of Senegal's tourism industry. By 1975, parastatal agencies controlled more than 40 percent of the value added in the modern sector and employed about one-third of the workers in the modern wage sector.

Some of Senegal's parastatal agencies and companies were much criticized because of mismanagement or widespread corruption. Western donors led by the World Bank criticized the inefficiency of the parastatals and their drain on public financial resources; the political opposition accused the regime of using the parastatals to pillage the country. The largest state agency and a frequent target of criticism was the Office National de Coopération et d'Assistance au Développement (National Office for Cooperatives and Development Assistance – ONCAD), which was established in 1966. At its height, ONCAD had more than 4,000 state employees and an annual turnover of approximately 100 billion francs CFA. ONCAD controlled all aspects of the internal marketing functions previously handled by the OCA and executed the state's agricultural program through the distribution of credit, seeds, fertilizer, and equipment to the rural population. The state used ONCAD to control the rural economy and to siphon resources from the rural to the urban sectors, thanks to the relatively low prices the Senegalese government paid the peanut farmer during the late 1960s and early 1970s. Over the years, ONCAD became increasingly unpopular with the peasantry. During the late 1970s, mismanagement and widespread corruption – high-ranking ONCAD officials were arrested for embezzling tens of millions of francs from ONCAD – also undermined its credibility with public opinion and foreign donors. On August 20, 1980, the Senegalese National Assembly voted to abolish ONCAD. Many of its extension service functions were then turned over to Regional Development Agencies (RDAs), and the cooperatives were permitted to sell their peanuts directly to the peanut oil industries without passing through an intermediary.

ONCAD was not the only parastatal to feel the ax. In the late 1970s, the government also dissolved other prominent but inefficient state companies, such as BUD-Sénégal, a nationalized agribusiness initially created to produce fruits and vegetables in Cap Vert for export to European markets using the most modern agricultural techniques; an enterprise set up to develop and manage a Senegalese tuna boat fleet; and a government well-digging company. During the early 1980s, the government was under heavy pressure to eliminate other costly and inefficient parastatal agencies as part of its economic recovery plan.

AFRICAN SOCIALISM, DEVELOPMENT
PLANNING, AND ECONOMIC POLICY

African Socialism has been Senegal's official ideology since independence. The African Socialism formulated by Mamadou Dia and Léopold Senghor stressed building a socialist society based on traditional African communitarian values and modern economic planning. African Socialism in the countryside was to be achieved through the development of the cooperative movement and the regrouping of Senegalese villages into self-governing rural communes.[13] Dia's blueprint for implementing African Socialism called for the revitalization of Senegal's 13,000 villages through the Rural Animation program (Animation Rurale) initiated by the state to democratize village institutions and local power structures and to mobilize the rural populations for developmental activities. The village-based multifunctional cooperative constituted the basic economic unit of the agrarian socialist society originally envisaged by Dia and Senghor. In the beginning the state would help organize the cooperatives and provide technical assistance. As the cooperatives gained more experience and managerial competence, they would extend their activities to encompass all aspects of production, marketing, credit, and distribution. In time, the village cooperatives would regroup into larger, more efficient cooperative unions, which would merge with the rural communes.

During the early 1960s, the government established a vast network of more than 1,600 cooperatives. Most of these were peanut marketing cooperatives. Dia's plan to expand the role of the cooperatives to conform with his socialist vision was dropped after his fall from power. During the mid-1960s, the cooperatives assumed responsibility for marketing Senegal's entire peanut crop. However, they did not evolve towards multifunctional autonomous economic development cells. Instead, they remained primarily channels for marketing peanuts and distributing agricultural credit and inputs in accordance with government-initiated programs. Most cooperatives came under the control of local party bosses, rural notables, or marabouts, who used the cooperatives for their own ends. The credibility of the cooperative movement was also undermined by the widespread corruption within ONCAD and the growing indebtedness of the cooperatives to the state. The peasants came to perceive the cooperatives as an instrument of oppression rather than of liberation and themselves as captives of the cooperatives.

Toward the end of the 1970s, some of the younger socialist cadres in government and the ruling party pressed for reforms to restore the

credibility of the cooperative movement and to give peasants more control over cooperative decision making. In 1980 some of these reforms
were implemented. It remains to be seen whether the coops will evolve
into the decentralized socialist institutions initially envisaged during the
early years of independence or will remain under the control of the central government and local elites.

As an ideology, African Socialism has affected Senegalese economic
policy in three important ways. First, it discouraged the emergence of
large-scale capitalist enterprises in the countryside and fostered the
development of rural cooperative structures rather than private plantations. In 1964 the Loi sur le Domaine National (National Domain Law)
gave the state proprietary rights over all rural land. Under this arrange-
ment, the state would be the steward of the land and allocate land rights
only to those who worked it. In theory, rents paid to absentee landlords
would be abolished; in practice, the government moved cautiously and
selectively in enforcing the law. Thus, Tukulor nobles in the Senegal
River valley still assert their traditional proprietary rights. One of the
most potentially explosive issues the government will have to face in the
future will be the allocation of land once the large-scale dams on the
Senegal River become operational.

Second, African Socialism's emphasis on the stewardship of the
state has been used to justify massive state intervention in regulating
and controlling key sectors of the Senegalese economy. Senghor regarded the state as the principal instrument for building the nation and a
socialist society. The state's role was to reconcile conflicting interests,
ensure social justice, and promote development. For their part, Marxist
critics of the regime have insisted that state intervention in Senegal is
a form of state capitalism rather than a manifestation of a socialist society.

Third, African Socialism did not insist upon the wholesale nationalization of all sectors of the economy. On the contrary, it was flexi-
ble enough to maintain that there was an important place for foreign
capital and the Senegalese private sector, provided that their activities
were compatible with national development goals. Senghor's stress on
dialogue, international cooperation, and the complementarity of civilizations emptied Senegalese African Socialism of the strident nationalist
content found in other hyphenated socialist ideologies. The identifica-
tion of Senegal's national leaders with the principles of European-style
democratic socialism since joining the Socialist International has made it
easier for the regime to justify its growing collaboration with foreign
capital and the Senegalese private sector. Democratic socialism is more
compatible with a mixed economy containing a strong if not dominant

private sector than is the African Socialism articulated by a Mamadou Dia who, since his release from prison in 1974, has become increasingly critical of Senegal's collaboration with foreign capital.[14]

A belief in the efficacy of national economic planning was another crucial component of African Socialism. During the early years of independence, the Senegalese four year plans incarnated the mystique of development promoted by the government. The First Plan (1961–1964) was elaborated under the supervision of Mamadou Dia after more than two years of careful study and preparation.[15] Dia worked closely with Father L. J. Lebret, a development specialist and cofounder of the French-based Economics and Humanism movement.[16] The First Four Year Plan provided an inventory of Senegal's resources and needs and was primarily concerned with qualitative goals and structural change. Hence, it stressed such goals as ending the isolation of the so-called peripheral regions and their integration into the market economy, diversification of agriculture, exploitation of Senegal's mineral wealth, the promotion of several basic industries, and the establishment of innovative state rural development agencies designed to mobilize the rural populations and provide them with technical assistance.

After ousting Dia in the middle of the First Plan, Senghor promised that Senegal would continue to pursue the priorities laid down by Mamadou Dia, except more efficiently. During the course of the First Plan, peanut production rose substantially, road-building projects made the Fleuve and the Casamance more accessible during the rainy season, and the state established a rural development bureaucracy that reached most of the country. However, little was done to diversify agriculture, and industrial growth was hampered by the loss of Senegal's former West African markets.

Although in some ways an extension of the First Plan, Senegal's Second Plan (1965–1969) was more project-oriented and placed much greater emphasis on raising production and productivity. In contrast with the frequent references to socialism in the First Plan, the Second Plan hardly mentioned the word. During this period, the Senghor government adopted a more "productionist" approach to rural development and downgraded the role to be played by some of the rural development institutions—the Rural Expansion Centers, Rural Animation, and the cooperative movement—established under Dia to spark economic development and African Socialism in the countryside. The Second Plan gave French technical assistance agencies the primary responsibility for improving productivity in the peanut zones and introducing new cash crops, such as cotton. Little was done to promote food crops outside the peanut basin. The Second Plan also liberalized the

Figure 3.3. M'Bao oil refinery, Cap Vert. One of Senegal's first basic industries. (Photo by Michel Renaudeau)

investment code to encourage more foreign investment industry, while tariff barriers were maintained to protect Senegal's import-substitution industries. Drought set back efforts to raise production in the peanut basin, and lower peanut prices further depressed the rural economy. As a result, the modest gains made in the industrial sector were more than canceled out by the decline of the agricultural sector.

Except for greater emphasis on promoting tourism, the Third Plan (1969–1973) maintained the same basic orientations as the Second Plan. The Third Plan coincided with periods of chronic drought that convinced the government that it had to make a greater effort to diversify the economy and reduce the country's vulnerability to drought. This moved the government to formulate plans for a series of *"grands projets"* (large-scale projects) that would permit the economy once and for all to break out of its dependency upon the peanut. This new approach required a massive influx of foreign aid and capital and centered around the following six projects: (1) the creation of a customs-free industrial zone to promote export-oriented industries; (2) the development of a giant oil refinery and petrochemical industry to service all of West Africa; (3) the rapid expansion of Dakar's port facilities to accommodate giant tankers and the establishment of a tanker-repair industry (Dakar-Marine);

(4) the expansion of Senegalese phosphate production and exports, intensification of the search for oil, and the exploitation of iron ore reserves in Eastern Senegal; (5) the establishment of a major tourism industry, which would become an important source of foreign exchange; and (6) the transformation of Dakar into a world-class international trade and convention center.

The *grands projets* were incorporated into the Fourth Plan (1973-1977). The initial planning period was particularly difficult for planners because of the effects of drought and the worldwide wave of inflation. By this time, the Senegalese plan had become primarily an instrument for listing projects that might be funded by foreign donors rather than a coherent development strategy. During the course of the Fourth Plan, the Senegalese government began to place greater emphasis on food production, reforestation, and other measures to protect the environment. Several new RDAs were also established to stimulate food and livestock production.

In the Fifth Plan (1977-1981) Senegalese development strategy once again turned its attention to some of the qualitative planning objectives that had been neglected since the early 1960s. Thus, the Fifth Plan listed reducing regional economic disparities, raising nutritional and health standards, promoting local participation in economic decision making, and improving the lot of women as important priorities. During the late 1970s, the Senegalese government placed greater emphasis on irrigated agriculture and pushed for the creation of major dam projects as the only way in which Senegal and its Sahelian neighbors could overcome the effects of drought and provide the regular water supplies needed to fully develop their agricultural potential.

In the early 1980s, the Senegalese economy was still floundering under the weight of a rapidly deteriorating rural economy and massive foreign debt. Few of the *grands projets* had been fully implemented. Only the booming tourist industry had come close to fulfilling expectations. Senegal's customs-free industrial zone had attracted few foreign investors; the international trade center was not very profitable, despite the prestige it brought to Senegal; phosphate production and exports climbed slowly because of sluggish world market prices; Senegal's oil and iron ore resources were many years away from being exploited; the fall of the shah of Iran had temporarily dampened Senegalese plans to build a giant oil refinery and petrochemical industry (see Chapter 4); and the expansion of Dakar's port and tanker facilities had to be scaled down with the reopening of the Suez Canal. However, Senegal's prospects, although grim for the short run, look much better in the long run, as many of the *grands projets* may eventually become operational.

DEVELOPMENT FOR WHOM?

During the colonial era, the Senegalese economy was developed primarily for the benefit of the metropole and expatriate companies involved in the colonial economy. The gap between the material benefits accruing to expatriates working in Senegal and those earned by Senegalese in the modern sector was enormous. Non-Africans earned three times the wages and salaries of Senegalese holding similar kinds of jobs,[17] and nearly all the profits generated by Senegal's largest firms went to foreigners.

After more than two decades of independence, the expatriate community of businessmen, professionals, and technical assistance personnel – predominantly French, but in recent years more diverse – still constitutes the most privileged economic group in Senegal. As late as 1974, non-Africans received more than 28 percent of wages and salaries, even though they accounted for only 5 percent of the modern labor force.[18]

Despite the often-reiterated commitment of the Senghor regime to redistributive justice and raising the living standards of Senegal's impoverished rural masses, the main beneficiaries of Senegalese economic policies during the Senghor era were the members of the political-administrative elite and their allies in the private sector. The Africanization and nationalization programs, which reduced foreign control over certain sectors of the economy, favored a small number of Senegalese businessmen, managers, and professionals in the private sector; influential politicians; government ministers; high-level civil servants; university professors; and Senegalese cadres and businessmen working for the parastatals. This group was predominantly male, highly educated, politically well connected, and able to afford European-style living standards – i.e., having a car, modern appliances, a nice villa or apartment, and opportunities to travel abroad. Although its size and influence has grown steadily since the 1970s, this group still constitutes only a tiny fraction of the total population and probably less than 5 percent of the urban population.

While there has been a modest shift in income distribution from foreigners to Senegalese nationals, the gap between the Senegalese elite and the masses has probably widened since independence. Thus, the annual income of the average peasant was less than one-twentieth that of Senegalese belonging to the most favored socioeconomic categories during the late 1970s.[19] And the salaries of high-ranking civil servants were generally five times those of government workers at the bottom of the public-sector wage scale. Since 1974, the government has made a greater effort to reduce the gap between town and countryside by transferring more resources from the urban sectors to the rural sectors.

Table 3.1
Socioeconomic indicators of the development gap between urban and
rural Senegal

Socioeconomic Indicators	Cap Vert	Rest of Country
Per capita income	$850-$1000	$75-$150
Percentage of GDP	55.2	44.8
Percentage of industrial enterprises	80.0	20.0
Daily calories per capita	2,535	2,070
Doctors per 10,000 inhabitants	2.4	0.2
Percentage of school-age children in school	60.6	22.0

Sources: Republic of Senegal, Cinquième Plan Quadriennal (1977-
1981) [Fifth four-year plan (1977-1981)] (Dakar: Nouvelles Editions
Africaines, 1977), pp. 22, 23, 65, 70; and Le Sénégal en chiffres,
éditions 1978 [Senegal in figures, 1978 edition] (Dakar: Société
Africaine d'Editions, 1979), pp. 113, 126.

On the whole, postcolonial development policies have failed to
raise living standards for most Senegalese or to redistribute wealth and
services in favor of the poor. Although Senegal's industrial development
strategy stimulated annual industrial growth rates of 5-7 percent during
the 1960s, it failed to prevent a significant decline in the real income of
the urban working class or to provide adequate employment opportunities for the country's rapidly growing labor force. Thus, wage
stabilization policies froze the minimum wage for much of the decade
and eroded African urban living standards, while the capital-intensive
technologies adopted by Senegal's new and older modernizing industries
created little new employment. During the 1970s and early 1980s, increases in the official minimum wage were offset by inflation and the
reduction of government subsidies for basic foodstuffs, such as rice,
bread, peanut oil, tomato sauce, and other essential consumer items.

In the countryside, rural development policies did little to alleviate
rural poverty, despite the government's efforts to raise production and
productivity through the diffusion of modern agricultural equipment
and technology. Thus far, the main beneficiaries have been the
bureaucrats, managers, technicians, and foreign technical assistance personnel involved in rural development agencies and programs and a small
number of marabouts, rural notables, and relatively wealthy farmers
with enough land and labor to take advantage of the modern equipment,
technology, and access to easy credit offered by the government. On the

other hand, the real incomes of most Senegalese farmers have dropped since the mid-1960s, and even farmers involved in relatively successful projects find themselves increasingly dependent upon state agencies and earning a relatively small return on their investment.[20] The combination of depressed peanut prices and drought contributed to a drastic decline in rural incomes during the late 1960s and early 1970s. Although the government has shifted more resources to the rural sectors since 1974 through higher producer prices, subsidies for agricultural inputs, and the expansion of agricultural extension services, real rural incomes have not kept up with inflation. When corrected for inflation, peanut prices are lower now than at independence. Thus, the 50 francs CFA per kilo received by the Senegalese peanut farmer during the 1980-1981 season was worth a third less than the 22 francs CFA per kilo he received two decades earlier.

In view of the negative growth rate in real per capita income since independence, it is rather remarkable that the living standards of Senegal's urban and rural masses have not fallen more than they have. Their relative well-being can be partially explained by the regime's responsiveness to popular economic discontent and a concern for carrying out wage and pricing policies aimed at preserving minimal living standards. Thus, the government has periodically raised the SMIG (*Salaire Minimum Interprofessionnelle Guaranti*), or minimum wage, to permit unskilled workers to more or less keep up with inflation and has kept down the cost of living for the urban poor by subsidizing the price of basic commodities. The misery of the rural masses during periods of drought was partially alleviated through large-scale food relief programs. Money from relatives working in France and in Dakar and other large African cities helped sustain rural living standards. In 1980 a "solidarity tax" equivalent to six days' wages was levied on urban wages to finance government relief programs for peasants and herders suffering from the latest drought; in 1981, this tax was doubled.[21] Foreign aid has provided the government with much-needed resources to prevent further declines in mass living standards. It has also permitted the regime to expand the state bureaucracy and maintain the privileges of the political-administrative elite.

During the late 1970s, growing dissatisfaction over deteriorating economic conditions and the privileges and ostentatious lifestyles of the Senegalese elite prompted the Senghor regime to place greater emphasis on equity and social justice in its economic programs. These concerns were expressed in Senegal's Fifth Development Plan (1977–1981). By the end of the decade, the government had increased its efforts to provide more basic services – wells, medicines, schools, and youth centers – for the rural populations. And in 1980, his last year in office, Senghor affirmed the government's intention to eliminate free housing and other perquisites previously enjoyed by ministers and other top government officials and to reduce the disparity in civil service pay scales by raising wages at the bottom end of the scale more rapidly than those at the top.

Since becoming president, Abdou Diouf has insisted that his regime will continue this commitment to social justice and the austerity programs he initiated while still prime minister. To demonstrate his sincerity, Diouf launched a major campaign against government corruption — *"l'enrichissement illicite"*—that led to the arrest and prosecution of several high-ranking government officials and put the fear of God into many others. It remains to be seen whether the Senegalese elite will accept its fair share of the hardships and belt-tightening that the government's IMF-inspired austerity policies will impose on the nation for much of the 1980s.

NOTES

1. It is extremely difficult to accurately estimate Senegal's per capita income and translate this figure into dollars. Sharply fluctuating exchange rates play havoc with such attempts. The official currency of Senegal is the CFA franc, which is tied to the French franc (1 French franc = 50 francs CFA). In the past decade, the value of the CFA franc in relation to the dollar has fluctuated between 200 and 310 francs CFA to the dollar. Efforts to compare changes in per capita income over time are further complicated by changes in official population statistics and high inflation rates.

2. For a detailed description of agrarian structures in Sahelian Senegal, see Paul Pélissier's monumental study, *Les paysans du Sénégal: Les civilisations agraires du Cayor à la Casamance* [Peasants of Senegal: Agrarian civilizations from Cayor to the Casamance] (Saint-Yrieix: Imprimerie Fabrèque, 1966) and Valy-Charles Diarrasouba, *L'évolution des structures agricoles du Sénégal* [The evolution of Senegalese agricultural structures] (Paris: Editions Cujas, 1968).

3. For a detailed analysis of Senegalese class structures, see Majhemout Diop, *Histoire des classes sociales dans l'Afrique de l'Ouest: Le Sénégal* [History of social classes in West Africa: Senegal] (Paris: François Maspero, 1972).

4. Most of the statistics presented in this chapter are taken directly or indirectly from official Senegalese sources. For the most recent and complete compendium of Senegalese statistics, see *Le Sénégal en chiffres, éditions 1978* [Senegal in figures, 1978 edition] (Dakar: Société Africaine d'Editions, 1978). For more recent statistical data see the quarterly reports on Senegalese economic indicators published by the Banque Centrale des Etats de l'Afrique de l'Ouest (Central Bank of West African States — BCEAO), based on the latest official Senegalese statistics.

5. For a useful collection of essays on Senegalese dependency, see Rita Cruise O'Brien, ed., *The Political Economy of Underdevelopment: Dependence in Senegal* (Beverly Hills, Calif.: Sage Publications, 1979).

6. On this point, see Samir Amin, *L'Afrique de l'Ouest bloquée* [The blocking of West African development] (Paris: Editions de Minuit, 1971), pp. 23–64.

7. For a detailed discussion of Dia's measures to "nationalize" the peanut

trade, see Edward J. Schumacher, *Politics, Bureaucracy, and Rural Development in Senegal* (Berkeley: University of California Press, 1975), pp. 131–149.

8. In 1964 the BSD absorbed the Credit Populaire du Sénégal, which provided short- and medium-term credit to Senegalese artisans, merchants, fishermen, and consumers, and was renamed the Banque Nationale du Développement Sénégalais (Senegalese National Development Bank – BNDS).

9. For example, see Rita Cruise O'Brien, "Foreign Ascendance in the Economy and State: The French and the Lebanese," in Rita Cruise O'Brien, *Political Economy of Underdevelopment*, pp. 100–125.

10. For a detailed description and analysis of this class, see Samir Amin, *Le monde des affaires sénégalais* [The Senegalese business world] (Paris: Editions de Minuit, 1969).

11. World Bank, *Senegal: Tradition, Diversification, and Economic Development* (Washington, D.C.: World Bank, 1974), p. 53.

12. For an analysis of the evolution of the parastatals, see Jean-Claude Gautron, "Les entreprises publiques, acteur et indicateur du changement social" [Public enterprises: Actors and indicators of social change], *Revue Française d'Etudes Politiques Africaines*, No. 188 (February 1979):43–62.

13. See Sheldon Gellar, Robert Charlick, and Yvonne Jones, *Animation Rurale and Rural Development: The Experience of Senegal* (Ithaca, N.Y.: Cornell University Rural Development Committee, 1980), pp. 34–103, for a discussion of the role of coops and rural animation in Senegalese African Socialism.

14. See Dia's frequent columns and editorials in *Andë Sopi*, a monthly opposition newspaper edited by the former prime minister.

15. For an extensive analysis of Senegal's planning process and the First Four Year Plan, see Sheldon Gellar, "The Politics of Development in Senegal," Ph.D. dissertation, Columbia University, 1967, p. 252–262. For a detailed analysis of the evolution of Senegalese planning since then, see Adama Diallo, "Planification en Afrique et modèle du développement sénégalais" [The Senegalese development model and planning in Africa], in Louis-Vincent Thomas, ed., *Prospective du développement en Afrique noire, un scenario: Le Sénégal* [Development prospective in Black Africa, a scenario: The Senegal case] (Paris: Presses Universitaires de France, 1978), pp. 47–65.

16. For a detailed discussion of Lebret and his work, see Denis Goulet, "Lebret: Pioneer of Development Ethics," in his *A New Moral Order: Studies in Development Ethics and Liberation Theology* (Maryknoll, N.Y.: Orbis Books, 1974), pp. 23–49.

17. For a detailed discussion of wage differentials and the reasons for these, see Guy Pfefferman, *Industrial Labor in the Republic of Senegal* (New York: Frederick A. Praeger, 1968).

18. *Le Sénégal en chiffres*, p. 71.

19. This point was made in a speech by Senghor before the Economic and Social Council in March 1979 in which he cited the efforts his government was making to narrow the income gap.

20. For a sharp critique of a state development agency's relationships with peasants involved in a rural development project, see Adrian Adams, "The Senegal River Valley: What Kind of Changes?" *Review of African Political Economy*, No. 10 (September-December 1977):33–59.

21. *Marchés Tropicaux*, May 1, 1981, p. 1243.

4

Senegal and the World

Senegal's small population and lack of wealth have not deterred it from becoming one of the most active and influential Black African countries on the international scene.[1] Since independence Senegal has developed ties with representatives of every major political and economic bloc in the world,[2] while Senegalese diplomats have played prominent roles in various regional and international organizations.

Although not formally aligned with any bloc of nations, Senegal has pursued a pro-Western foreign policy. This can be seen in Senegal's special relationship with France, its preference for ties with the West, its position as a leader of the moderate francophone Black African states, and its staunch opposition to Soviet and Cuban intervention in Africa.

Senegal has made its presence felt in African, Islamic, and Third World politics. During the Senghor era,[3] Senegalese diplomacy was remarkably successful in staying on good terms with contending ideological camps and nations. Thus, Senegal developed close ties with Anwar Sadat and Egypt while retaining cordial relationships with Yassir Arafat and the Palestine Liberation Organization (PLO). As a member of the forty-two-nation Islamic Conference, Senegal intensified its ties to the Muslim World and became increasingly critical of Israeli policy. As a nonaligned Third World nation, Senegal has been one of the most articulate advocates of a New International Economic Order (NIEO), has supported anticolonial and national liberation movements in Portugal's African colonies and Southern Africa, and has opposed superpower intervention in Vietnam, Angola, and Afghanistan.

THE FRENCH CONNECTION

After more than two decades of independence, Senegal's special relationship with France remains the cornerstone of its foreign policy. The French connection is deeply rooted in modern Senegalese history. French political, economic, and cultural institutions were implanted in Senegal as far back as the seventeenth century with the establishment of

67

Saint Louis as the capital of French Senegal. Senegal's privileged position within the French colonial system and the involvement of Senegalese intellectuals and politicians in metropolitan politics and culture have left cultural and emotional bonds that are not easily broken. Senegalese intellectuals still read *Le Monde* regularly and closely follow the political debates raging in the French press. Left-wing Senegalese critics of Senegal's "neocolonial" ties with France often launch their attacks in the language and style of the French left.[4] At the same time, it is not unusual for Senegalese government leaders to angrily dismiss personal criticism and attacks on the Senegalese government and its policies appearing in the French press as manifestations of neocolonialism, paternalism, or subtle forms of racism.[5] Senegal's special relationship with France during the Senghor era (1960–1980) was reinforced by Senghor's personal loyalty to France and his acceptance of most of the premises of Gaullist foreign policy.[6] Like the French, Senghor thus opposed the domination of world politics by the two major superpowers, regarded France as the natural leader of an independent Europe and a champion of Third World interests, and saw an alliance between Europe and Africa as the best hope for providing a "Third Force" to counteract superpower domination. With the emergence of the Organization of Petroleum Exporting Countries (OPEC), Senghor's vision of a Third Force expanded to include the oil-producing nations of the Middle East. While still in office, Senghor worked closely with France to promote a *"trilogue"* among Europe, Africa, and the Middle East,[7] a policy Senegal still pursues vigorously under the direction of Senghor's successor. Senghor was also one of the chief exponents of a loose commonwealth of French-speaking nations—*la francophonie*—joined together by common cultural and linguistic bonds. It is doubtful that future Senegalese leaders will share as strong a personal attachment and loyalty to France as Senghor, who spent most of his young adult life in France, served in the French army, and fought in the French resistance during World War II.

Economic dependency on France is another crucial factor underlying Senegal's close ties with France. Although France no longer monopolizes Senegalese foreign trade and aid as it did at independence, the former metropole remains Senegal's principal trading partner and most important source of financial and technical assistance. France has been willing to finance projects and in areas that other donors have not been willing or able to enter. And when the Senegalese government finds itself in a serious financial bind, it usually turns to France for help. For example, Prime Minister Abdou Diouf went to Paris in July 1980 to seek an emergency loan to permit the Senegalese government to meet its payroll and pay off its major domestic suppliers, thus averting the closing of many firms and a dramatic rise in unemployment. France responded promptly with a 21 billion francs CFA loan.[8] Finally, Senegal's membership in the franc zone ties its economy closely to France.

Since independence Franco-Senegalese relationships have gone through three different phases. The first phase was dominated by the presence of Charles de Gaulle, who insisted upon maintaining paternalistic relationships with Senegal and other former French Black African colonies remaining in the French orbit. De Gaulle promised to provide generous financial and technical assistance in exchange for their fidelity to France and to protect the new francophone states against internal subversion and hostile neighbors. During the Gaullist years, Senegal did little to reduce its economic dependency upon France or to Africanize French-held sectors of the economy. On the contrary, Senghor often deplored the reluctance of metropolitan firms to invest in Senegal and expressed the fear that French public opinion was succumbing to Cartierism[9] and was less willing to support aid programs to France's former colonies.

The upheavals of May–June 1968 that rocked France and the Gaullist regime also spread to Senegal. The agitation and unrest in Dakar during this period was in large part triggered by popular resentment over French political, economic, and cultural domination. France stood by Senghor during the crisis. Although both de Gaulle and Senghor survived the upheavals, the end of the Gaullist era was near. De Gaulle's departure from the political scene in April 1969 signaled the beginning of a new phase in Franco-Senegalese relationships.

Under Georges Pompidou (1969–1974), de Gaulle's successor, France showed more flexibility and less paternalism in dealing with the francophone African states. Senegal continued to enjoy warm relations with France, abetted by Senghor's long-time friendship with Pompidou dating back to the 1920s, when both men had been students at the prestigious Louis Le Grand Lycée in Paris. The 1974 revisions of the postindependence Franco-Senegalese cooperation agreements reduced the size of the French military contingent in Senegal, transferred Senegalese military bases from French to Senegalese sovereignty, and stepped up the Africanization of the University of Dakar. These were all measures long demanded by Senegalese nationalists, and their implementation provided tangible signs of the evolution away from the paternalism of the past.

The election of Valéry Giscard d'Estaing to the French presidency following Pompidou's death in 1974 opened a third phase in Franco-Senegalese ties. Giscard continued to pursue a Gaullist policy in Africa and to maintain the annual Franco-African summits that had been ini-

Figure 4.1. Senghor and former French President Giscard d'Estaing review Senegalese troops. (Photo by Michel Renaudeau)

tiated by Pompidou in 1973. During the late 1970s, Senegalese foreign policy became more intertwined with that of France. Thus, Senegal supported French military intervention in Chad, applauded France's role in ousting the Bokassa regime in the Central African Empire, permitted France to use Senegalese air bases, and joined forces with France and Morocco in sending troops to Zaire to defend Shaba Province against invasion by rebel forces opposing the Mobutu regime. Senegal's growing ties with the Islamic world have also made Senegal's friendship a valuable asset to France in its pursuit of greater influence and secure oil supplies in the Middle East.

A few months after Senghor's departure, the defeat of Giscard d'Estaing and the coming to power of François Mitterrand and the French Socialists signaled the beginning of a new phase in Franco-Senegalese relations. The Diouf regime welcomed the unexpected Socialist victory in the 1981 French national elections. As a member of the Socialist International, the PS had established close ties with Mitterrand and other French Socialist leaders. Senegal enthusiastically supported Mitterrand's pro–Third World foreign policies and commitment to increase French aid to Black Africa. For its part, the French Socialist regime warmly praised Senegal's human rights record and efforts to promote democracy and regarded Senegal as one of its staunchest and most reliable allies in Black Africa. Thus, Senegal continued to maintain its special relationship with France during the early 1980s, thanks to the ideological affinities and past party ties linking the PS to the French Socialists.

While Senegal's special relationship with France continues, the French presence itself in Senegal has been declining steadily since independence.[10] Thus, the number of French living in Senegal dropped from nearly 40,000 in 1960 to less than 18,000 by the beginning of the 1980s. The drastic reduction in the number of French administrative and military personnel immediately after independence; Senegal's stagnant economy; greater economic opportunities for Europeans in the Ivory Coast, Cameroon, and Gabon; and the Africanization of skilled-labor and managerial jobs in the private sector were all factors contributing to the decline in the number of French living in Senegal.

SENEGAL AND AFRICA

During the Gaullist 1960s, Senegal's inter-African foreign policy focused primarily on its relationships with its immediate neighbors and other francophone states in North and Black Africa. In the 1970s, however, Senegal dramatically expanded its diplomatic horizons and became much more involved in continental African politics as it developed close ties with Zaire, Egypt, and other African states traditionally outside the French sphere of influence, opposed Soviet and Cuban intervention in Angola and Ethiopia, and resisted Libyan efforts to gain a foothold in Black Africa.

Despite its extensive involvement in African diplomacy, Senegal has often felt isolated within its own immediate region. For many years, Senegal was rarely able to enjoy good relations with all its neighbors at the same time. However, by the end of the 1970s the situation had improved.

Senegal's relations with Mali hit bottom during the early 1960s after the collapse of the Mali Federation in August 1960. Mali broke its ties with Senegal and rerouted its trade through the Ivory Coast even though the Dakar-Niger railroad provided the most economical way of shipping goods in and out of landlocked Mali. Relations between the two countries began to improve in 1965 when Mali agreed to cooperate with Senegal in the development of the Senegal River basin. Economics brought the two countries closer together during the 1970s. Both countries realized that they had to cooperate in order to attract the tens of millions of dollars needed to finance the Diama and Manantali dam projects. The Malians are counting on the Manantali dam to provide massive amounts of hydroelectric power and an outlet to the sea for their landlocked country. Senegal saw the dams as a safeguard against drought and an instrument for achieving national food self-sufficiency.

During the Senghor era, Senegal's relations with Guinea were frequently stormy. As one of the leaders of the radical camp in Africa, Guinea clashed with Senegal on many issues concerning the decolonization of Africa. Led by the fiery Sékou Touré, Guinea invariably took a more militant anticolonialist position than Senegal, which it often accused of being an instrument of French neocolonialism. Another major source of conflict was the fact that Senegal gave political refuge to tens of thousands of Guineans fleeing their country. Relations between Senegal and Guinea deteriorated rapidly after Touré smashed an unsuccessful attempt to overthrow his regime by an invasion launched from Portuguese Guinea in November 1970. Guinea accused Senegal of training some of the rebels involved in the invasion and colluding with France and Portugal to overthrow the regime. Senegal denied the charges and refused to meet Guinea's request to send Guinean political exiles living in Senegal back to Guinea. The two countries then launched vitriolic radio attacks on each other's regimes. The "battle of the airwaves" continued for several years, reaching its peak in 1973 when Senegal broke off diplomatic relations with Guinea.

Senegalese-Guinean relationships improved dramatically following Guinea's rapprochement with France in 1978. That same year a reconciliation between Touré and his two arch-rivals, Senghor and Houphouët-Boigny, took place in Monrovia. Senghor and Touré formally buried the hatchet in October 1979 during a state visit by the Guinean president to Senegal.[11] Relations between Senegal and Guinea continued to improve during the early 1980s as Touré took steps to liberalize his regime, moved closer to France, and became more active in the Islamic Conference. Common development problems also brought Senegal and Guinea together. The Senegal and Gambia rivers both rise in Guinea, and Guinean cooperation is needed to exploit the full potential of the rivers. In 1981 Guinea joined the Organisation de Mise en Valeur du Fleuve Gambie (Organisation for the Development of the Gambia River Basin – OMVG), which had been created in 1978 by Senegal and Gambia.

Unlike Mali, Mauritania showed little interest in federating with Senegal at independence.[12] Its Arab-speaking Moorish majority tended to identify more with the Arab Islamic world than with francophone Black Africa. During the early 1960s, Senegal and other francophone Black African states supported Mauritania in the face of Moroccan claims that Mauritania was an integral part of Morocco. During the late 1960s, Senegalese-Mauritanian relations cooled when Mauritania began to loosen its ties with the francophone African bloc and move closer to the Arab world. Mauritania joined the Arab League in 1973. As Senegal itself developed closer ties with the Islamic world, relations between the two countries again improved. Senegal supported Mauritania's claim to that part of Spanish Sahara which it annexed in 1975 and backed both Mauritania and Morocco in their conflict with the Polisario liberation movement. Relations again cooled after the military government that took power in Mauritania in 1978 made its peace with Polisario in 1979 while Senegal continued to support Morocco. In early 1981, an unsuccessful attempt at a military coup launched by Mauritanian exiles and backed by Morocco led to charges by Mauritania that Senegal had been involved in the plot. President Diouf denied the charges and expelled Mauritanian opponents of the regime living in Senegal.

One potential source of conflict between the two countries is the dissatisfaction of large segments of Mauritania's Black African minority concentrated along the Senegal River with the Arabization programs imposed by the Moorish majority since independence. The French-educated Tukulor elite has led the fight against Arabization, which it sees as reducing the Black African minority to second-class status. Although ethnic and communal conflicts between Moor and Tukulor pose a threat to Mauritanian national unity, they have not yet become a major bone of contention between Senegal and Mauritania. But it could well become an explosive problem in the future if Tukulor nationalists should call upon Senegal to support their demands for greater autonomy.

Like Mali and Senegal, Mauritania stands to benefit from the construction of the Diama and Manantali dams. Mauritania seeks to reduce its massive food deficits by developing irrigated agriculture on its side of the Senegal River. However, Mauritania has been less enthusiastic than Senegal in promoting Senegal River basin development because of fears that greater economic integration of its black populations with Senegal might encourage separatist tendencies.

For many years, Senegal's relations with Guinea-Bissau were colored by Senegal's stance toward Portugal and the liberation forces during the long drawn-out war for national independence (1963–1974). Senghor's efforts to persuade Portugal to negotiate a peaceful withdrawal from Portuguese Guinea during the early 1960s failed. When the armed struggle led by Amilcar Cabral and the African Independence Party of Guinea and Cap Vert (PAIGC) broke out in 1963, the Senegalese at first supported a rival group. As the war intensified, thousands of refugees crossed the border into the Casamance. Portugal's raids and shelling of Senegalese border villages severely strained relations between Senegal and Portugal during the late 1960s and early 1970s. Senegal responded by sending military units to the Casamance to patrol the border and asking the UN Security Council in November 1971 to condemn Portuguese violations of Senegal's national sovereignty and territorial integrity. Although sympathetic to the liberation struggle, Senegal moved to restrict the movement and training of Guinean freedom fighters on Senegalese soil. These measures did not endear Senegal to Cabral and the PAIGC. However, when Guinea-Bissau declared its independence in 1974, Senegal was one of the first African countries to recognize the new nation. Since then, Senegal's relations with Guinea-Bissau have improved. Senegal's initial concern that the presence of the more radical regime in neighboring Guinea-Bissau might stimulate autonomist movements in the Casamance proved to be unfounded because of Guinea-Bissau's own internal political problems and preoccupation with rebuilding its war-torn economy. When the Luiz Cabral government was overthrown by Nino Vieyra in November 1980, Senegal moved quickly to recognize the new regime.

Of all its immediate neighbors, Senegal today enjoys its best relationships with the Gambia. This was not always the case. When the Gambia obtained its independence from Great Britain in 1965, many observers felt that the tiny country would soon be absorbed by its larger neighbor. However, the Gambia resisted Senegalese efforts to establish a formal Senegambian confederation because the English-speaking Gambian elite feared being swallowed up by Senegal. During the late 1960s and early 1970s, Senegal accused the Gambia of "economic aggression" because of the large-scale smuggling that took place across Senegal-Gambia borders. At that time, many Senegalese peanut farmers unhappy with the low peanut prices in Senegal sold their peanuts in the Gambia. Smuggling of consumer goods, such as transistor radios and watches, deprived the Senegalese government of revenues derived from taxes levied on imported goods, while Senegal's infant textile industry suffered from the large volume of cheap Asian textiles smuggled into Senegal from the Gambia.

Since the mid-1970s, the two countries have moved closer to each other, especially in the areas of economic cooperation and foreign policy. In 1978 Senegal and the Gambia formed the OMVG, and in 1980, the two countries agreed to build a combination bridge and antisalt dam across the Gambia. When completed sometime in the mid-1980s, the bridge will eliminate a major bottleneck to the Casamance's economic integration with northern Senegal and stimulate more trade between Senegal and the Gambia. Like Senegal, the Gambia under the leadership of Sir Dawda Jawara has intensified its links with the Islamic world and adopted similar stances on many international issues. In November 1980 Senegal sent troops to the Gambia at the request of the Gambian government, which reported that Libya was financing efforts to recruit Gambian nationals for military training in Libya to overthrow the present regimes in the Gambia and Senegal and establish Islamic republics.[13] On July 30, 1981, while President Jawara was in London to attend the wedding of Prince Charles and Lady Diana, left-wing elements seized power and proclaimed the establishment of a Marxist-Leninist regime in the Gambia. Jawara asked for help; Senegal responded immediately by sending troops and crushing the rebellion after several days of bloody fighting in Banjul, the Gambian capital. With Jawara restored to power, the two governments began negotiations to establish a confederation. By the end of the year, the Gambian and Senegalese governments ratified a treaty establishing the Senegambian confederation that went into effect on February 1, 1982.

One of the permanent features of Senegal's foreign policy since independence has been its efforts to build and sustain a coherent bloc of moderate francophone Black African states strong enough to play a major role in African continental politics. During the 1960s Senghor and Houphouët-Boigny of the Ivory Coast continued their old rivalry and vied for the leadership of the moderate francophone African states regrouped within the Organisation Commune Africaine et Malgache (Joint African and Malagasy Organization–OCAM). Houphouët saw OCAM primarily as a political instrument for combatting the influence of the more radical states within the Organization of African Unity (OAU) while Senghor looked to OCAM to promote economic cooperation and new markets for Senegalese exports. Because of the Ivory Coast's economic prosperity and dominant position within the Conseil de l'Entente, (Entente Council), a loose economic group consisting of the Ivory Coast, Upper Volta, Benin, and Niger, Houphouët-Boigny was in a much better position to assert a leadership role within OCAM than was Senghor.[14]

During the early 1970s, OCAM lost its cohesiveness as a unified pro-French political bloc. Several francophone African states withdrew from OCAM, and most of France's former colonies demanded a revision of the paternalistic Franco-African cooperation agreements drawn up at independence. While OCAM was fragmenting, Senghor and Houphouët-Boigny patched up their differences and formed a Dakar-Abidjan axis to isolate Guinea. Houphouët also agreed to support Senghor's plan to establish a West African Economic Community (CEAO) of francophone states in 1973. The CEAO brought together Senegal, Mali, Mauritania, the Ivory Coast, and Niger in a free-trade customs union that permitted Senegal to expand its trade with these countries and recapture some of the markets it had lost during the early 1960s.

Although wary of Nigeria's great size and new-found oil wealth, Senegal joined the Economic Community of West African States

Figure 4.2. Senegal and francophone West Africa. Senghor and his former rival Houphouët-Boigny lead a parade of francophone African leaders meeting in Dakar. (Photo by Michel Renaudeau)

(ECOWAS) founded in Lagos in 1975. After Senegal joined ECOWAS, Senghor called for an even broader Atlantic African economic community that would extend from Mauritania to Zaire and include all the francophone states of Central and Equatorial Africa. This, of course, would bring in more francophone states to counterbalance the weight of Nigeria. In the meantime, Senegal worked hard to reinforce the cohesion of the CEAO as a bloc within ECOWAS.

During the late 1970s, Senegal played an increasingly active role in francophone African politics and developed close ties with the Mobutu regime in Zaire. Senegal denounced the 1976 invasion of Shaba Province and sent a battalion of Senegalese troops to Zaire in June 1978 as part of an African peacekeeping force to defend the province against further attack. It took the lead in promoting a nonaggression and mutual defense pact among CEAO members, which was signed in Abidjan in 1977. Senegal has also played a leadership role at the Franco-African summit conferences that have taken place on a regular basis since 1973. The fourth Franco-African summit was held in Dakar in 1977. At the sixth Franco-African conference, held in Kigali in 1979, Senghor again called for the creation of a French-speaking commonwealth that would rival the English-speaking Commonwealth in influence and prestige and serve as a bridge between the industrialized and developing countries. It remains to be seen whether Diouf will pursue Senghor's concept of *"la francophonie"* with as much enthusiasm as his predecessor.

Senegal is tied to North Africa by history, religion, and culture. While president, Senghor often cited the many contributions of Berber and Arab culture to Black African civilization and insisted upon the need for Black Africa to maintain close ties with its White African neighbors in North Africa. During the first decade of independence, Senegal was primarily concerned with its relationships with Algeria, Morocco, and Tunisia.

Senegal and Tunisia had much in common. Both were pro-Western, had similar pluralistic one-party systems, claimed to be socialist, and although predominantly Muslim, did not share the bitterly anti-Israel outlook of Algeria, Libya, and the Arab states of the Middle East. Senghor worked very well with Habib Bourguiba, the Tunisian leader, and their friendship spanned the entire Senghor era. At the beginning of the 1980s Senegalese-Tunisian relations were as warm as they had been during the early 1960s. Both countries continued to work closely together as the leading members of the Inter-African Socialist Movement, created by Senghor during the late 1970s.

Throughout much of the Senghor era, Senegal and Algeria found themselves in opposite camps. One of the leaders of the radical camp within the OAU, Algeria was committed to radical social revolution at home and support of national liberation movements in those parts of Africa still under colonial rule during the 1960s. Senegal also supported national liberation movements, but it advocated more conciliatory approaches that stressed negotiations rather than armed struggle. Over the years, Algeria moved closer to the Soviet Union and other nations in the socialist camp in its foreign policy and attempted to assume a leadership role in Third World politics.

During Senghor's last years in office, Senegal and Algeria continued to take sharply different positions on several major issues. Thus, Senegal deplored the presence of Cuban troops on Angolan soil, refused to recognize the pro-Soviet regime in Angola, and denounced efforts by

Algeria, Angola, and Cuba to push the nonaligned Third World bloc into the socialist camp. Relations with Algeria improved considerably after Diouf took power.

Senegal has maintained close ties with Morocco since the mid-1960s, when Morocco renounced its claims on Mauritania and left the radical bloc in the OAU. Senegal applauded Franco-Moroccan military intervention in Zaire in 1976 and later supported Morocco in its attempts to put down the Algerian-backed Polisario movement during the late 1970s and early 1980s. In 1982 Senegal was working quietly to bring about a peaceful resolution of the Western Sahara conflict by promoting an OAU-sponsored referendum in the region claimed by Morocco.

One of the major developments of the 1970s was Senegal's growing involvement with Libya and Egypt in inter-African politics. During the late 1970s, Senegalese-Libyan relationships deteriorated rapidly because of Libyan intervention in Chad and the Kaddafi regime's backing of Ahmed Niasse's movement to overthrow the Senghor regime and replace it with a radical Islamic republic. Senegal also reacted strongly when the Goukouni government, which had gained power in Chad largely through Libyan military intervention, announced that Chad would soon hold a referendum to approve a proposed merger with Libya. In 1981 Senegal led a diplomatic offensive against Libya throughout francophone Africa, helped push through an OAU resolution condemning the proposed merger, and pressured France to take a stronger position against Libyan expansionism in Black Africa and reaffirm its obligation to defend its francophone African allies. When Libya moderated its stance and withdrew its troops from Chad in late 1981, tensions eased somewhat.

While emerging as one of the staunchest African opponents of Libya, Senegal was also drawing closer to Egypt. Senegal supported Sadat's Middle East peace initiatives and maintained its friendship with Egypt when Egypt became increasingly isolated in the Arab world following the signing of the Camp David agreements. Under Sadat, Egypt regarded Senegal as a valuable ally, helping Egypt to gain new friends in Black Africa and a more sympathetic hearing for Egypt's views on the Middle East within the European-dominated Socialist International. After Sadat's assassination in 1981, Senegal continued to maintain its strong ties with Egypt and worked discreetly behind the scenes to facilitate a reconciliation between Egypt and the moderate Arab states.

SENEGAL AND THE ISLAMIC WORLD

Despite its special relationship with France and its advocacy of a French-speaking commonwealth of nations, Senegal has still managed to establish its credentials as a prominent member of the Islamic world. Senegal's close ties with both the West and Islam continue patterns found in Senegal's colonial and precolonial past. They are also a product of a policy initiated by Senghor to make independent Senegal a bridge joining African, European, and Islamic civilizations.

During the early years of independence, Senegal's relations with the Arab Middle East were primarily a function of internal concerns. Senegal quickly established diplomatic relations with Saudi Arabia because of the need to facilitate the pilgrimage for the several thousand Senegalese who travel to Mecca each year to fulfill their religious obligations. Senegal's ties with Lebanon were initially motivated by the presence of West Africa's largest Lebanese community,[15] which had swelled to 20,000 people since the first Lebanese entrepreneurs came to Senegal toward the end of the nineteenth century. In the early 1960s Senegal did not take sides in the Arab-Israeli conflict. It enjoyed excellent relations with Israel, which was then widely regarded in Black Africa as a small, courageous developing country willing to share its technical expertise with the Third World. After the Six Day War, however, Senegal's friendship with Israel cooled and its foreign policy tilted toward the Arab side. When Israel rebuffed Senghor's peacemaking efforts as head of an OAU-sponsored mission to the Middle East in November 1971, Senegalese relations with Israel steadily deteriorated. Senegal demonstrated its sympathy for the Arab cause by permitting the PLO to open an office in Dakar in February 1973, the first PLO office in Black Africa. And in October 1973, Senegal joined several other Black African states in formally breaking diplomatic relations with Israel less than a month after the outbreak of the Yom Kippur War. During the early 1980s, Senegalese diplomacy stepped up its attacks on Israel as Senegal drew closer to the Arab world.

Economic considerations were another major factor spurring Senegal to strengthen its ties with the Islamic world. Hard-pressed by drought and soaring fuel prices following the 1973 Arab oil boycott, Senegal welcomed the financial assistance offered by the oil-rich Arab nations to Black Africa. Senegal appealed to Muslim religious solidarity in developing close ties with Saudi Arabia and Kuwait, conservative Muslim countries committed to promoting Islam throughout Black Africa. Saudi Arabia financed the creation of an Islamic Institute in Dakar and gave the Senegalese government millions of dollars in loans and grants, while Kuwait opened up a joint Senegalese-Kuwaiti Development Bank in Dakar. Other oil-rich Arab countries like Iraq, Abu Dhabi, and Qatar also provided extensive financial assistance. During the 1970s, the Arabs set up multilateral financial institutions like the Arab Bank for Economic Development in Africa and the Islamic Development Bank to disburse aid to friendly Muslim African states and to those supporting the Arab position in the Middle East. Between 1975 and 1979, Senegal received more than $60 million in bilateral and multilateral aid from Arab nations and institutions.[16]

Senegal did not limit its ties to the Islamic Middle East to the Arab countries; it also sought the patronage of the shah of Iran. While the Arab countries provided Senegal with money and religious instruction, Iran offered Senegal oil and capital for a billion-dollar petrochemical industry based on Iranian oil and Senegalese phosphates and a new ultra-modern port city to be named Keur Farah Pahlavi in honor of the shah's wife. Senegalese-Iranian relations expanded rapidly[17] after Senghor attended the twenty-five-hundredth anniversary of the Persian Empire in 1971. Senegal's blossoming partnership with Iran was further reinforced by Senghor's ties with Sadat, who was also a close friend of the shah. The partnership collapsed suddenly in 1979 when the Iranian Revolution drove the shah into exile. The Senegalese government kept its distance from the Khomeini regime because of its militant religious radicalism. When Iraq invaded Iran in 1981, Senegal, although it did not take sides, tended to be more sympathetic to Iraq.

Notwithstanding the loss of Iran as an ally, Senegalese diplomacy succeeded remarkably well in dealing with the rest of the Islamic world during the Senghor era. Despite Senegal's gravitation toward conservative Arab countries like Saudi Arabia and Kuwait, and its close ties with Egypt, Senegal has also managed to maintain friendly relations with the PLO and Iraq. Senegal pleased Saudi Arabia by calling for the liberation of Jerusalem from Israeli rule, Egypt by endorsing the aims of the Camp David agreements, and the PLO by vigorously advocating the Palestinian cause in the United Nations.

The prospects for even better relations with the Islamic world improved when the Muslim Diouf replaced the Catholic Senghor as Senegal's national leader. With its growing Islamic identity and need for Arab capital to finance major development projects, Senegal moved steadily closer to the Islamic world during the early 1980s.

SENEGAL AND THE THIRD WORLD

In pursuing an activist foreign policy, Senegal has been one of the most outspoken Black African nations demanding a revision of the Third World's economic relations with the industrialized countries. Senegalese leaders have blamed the deterioration of the terms of trade between Third World economies exporting raw materials and importing manufactured goods and capital from the developed countries as a major obstacle to Third World development. Senegal was one of the prime movers of the 1967 Algiers Conference, which prepared the way for the strong stand taken by the "Group of 77" at the 1968 UN Conference on Trade and Development (UNCTAD), held in New Delhi and cosponsored by Senegal and India. The Group of 77, which comprised most of the nations of Asia, Africa, and Latin America, demanded improved terms of trade for Third World primary products, preferential treatment for exports of Third World manufactures to developed countries, and increased financial aid from developed countries. These demands eventually became the basis for the NIEO requested by the Third World in 1974. In promoting the NIEO, Senegal called for dialogue, criticizing vituperation and direct confrontation with the richer nations as ineffective. While he was in power, Senghor insisted that the Third World could best obtain its goals by maintaining its unity on international economic issues and using the United Nations and other international forums to press the case for the NIEO.

Peaceful coexistence with different forms of political and economic systems has been a major principle of Senegalese foreign policy since independence. For example, in dealing with Asia, Senegal has taken great pains to maintain good relationships with communist countries such as the People's Republic of China, North Korea, Vietnam, and Kampuchea. It also astutely avoids taking sides in disputes involving contending Asian countries. As a result, Senegal has succeeded in maintaining diplomatic ties with both North and South Korea, China and Vietnam, Pakistan and Bangladesh. Its ties with Asian communist nations give credibility to Senegal's claim to nonaligned status despite its clear preference for the West.

Senegalese diplomacy has been far less active in Latin America, where cultural and economic concerns have been more important than political ones. During the 1970s, Senghor made several goodwill trips to Latin American countries, including Brazil, Argentina, Mexico, Venezuela, and Costa Rica. On the other hand, Senegal's relations with Cuba have been poor since the latter's military involvement in Angola and Ethiopia during the middle and late 1970s.

Senegalese diplomats have been very active in the UN. For more than a decade, a Senegalese, Amadou Moktar M'Bow has served as secretary-general of the United Nations Educational, Scientific and Cultural Organization (UNESCO), which has been recently promoting a New International Information Order in which Third World countries would have a greater voice in controlling the dissemination of news about their countries, which is now dominated by Western news agencies. Senegal has often spoken out on many issues of concern to the Third World in UN forums—the arms race, the need for an NIEO, condemnation of the apartheid regime in South Africa, and so on. Senegal also sent troops to Lebanon in 1978 as part of a UN peacekeeping operation. At the September 1979 summit meeting of nonaligned nations held in Havana, Senegal was the most outspoken critic of Cuban pressures to push the Third World closer to the Soviet Union.

SENEGAL AND EAST-WEST RELATIONSHIPS

One major aim of Senegalese foreign policy since independence has been to keep the Cold War out of Africa. Senegal wants both the United States and the Soviet Union to refrain from meddling in the internal affairs of African states or taking sides in inter-African disputes. As a nonaligned Third World nation, Senegal has criticized the United States's Vietnam policies and Soviet military intervention in Afghanistan. Closer to home, Senegal has denounced the stationing of Cuban troops and Soviet military advisers in Angola and Ethiopia and chided the United States for dragging its feet in seeking to end white minority rule in Southern Africa. Senegal has carefully avoided taking a partisan position in the political struggle between the two superpowers. Hence, although it condemned the Soviet invasion of Afghanistan, Senegal did not follow the U.S. lead in boycotting the 1980 Olympic games held in Moscow, on the grounds that sports should be separated from politics and not be used as a pawn in the Cold War.

Although officially nonaligned, Senegal is clearly closer to the West than to the Soviet Union and Eastern Europe in its political and economic outlook. Within the West, Senegal looks more toward Western Europe than toward the United States. And in dealing with Europe's communist states, Senegal enjoys much warmer relations with Yugoslavia and Romania than with the Soviet Union and its Eastern European satellites.

While maintaining its special relationship with France, Senegal has also reached out to other Western European nations. During the 1960s, Senegal dealt primarily with the EEC, which then consisted of the "Six" — France, West Germany, Italy, Belgium, the Netherlands, and Luxembourg. Senegal's association with the EEC facilitated an influx of non-French consumer goods as tariff barriers were lowered and brought in a new source of development loans and grants from the European Development Fund, which partially compensated for a decline in French aid after independence. Senegal and other francophone African nations count heavily upon France to champion their cause within the EEC by lobbying for more aid and preferential tariff treatment for the associated African states. For their part, France's EEC partners were not particularly eager to become more generous toward the African states because they saw France as the main beneficiary.

When the EEC was enlarged in 1972 to include Great Britain and other Western European nations that had not previously joined, Senegal widened its European contacts by signing economic and cultural agreements with the Scandinavian countries, Switzerland, Spain, and Portugal. At the same time, Senegal reinforced its bilateral ties with Great Britain and West Germany. Politically, Senghor increased Senegal's visibility and influence in European circles after the PS joined the Socialist International, which brought Senegalese political leaders into more frequent and regular contact with socialist parties throughout Western Europe. Senegal's extensive links with many Western European countries have enhanced its reputation in Europe and increased the number of Senegal's aid and trade partners. However, despite the diversification of Senegal's European ties, France and the "Six" continue to be Senegal's main trading partners and sources of foreign aid, accounting for nearly two-thirds of the country's foreign aid and trade.

Senegal's diplomatic relations with the United States date back to the early 1960s. Senegal was one of the first African countries to accept U.S. Peace Corps volunteers, and Senegal enjoyed especially good relations with the United States during the Kennedy era. The Vietnam War did little to enhance the popularity of the United States in Senegal. Nor did the assassinations of Martin Luther King, Jr., and Robert Kennedy in the spring of 1968.

U.S. interest in Senegal increased after the establishment of the Sahel Development Program in 1973 as the United States stepped up its food and economic aid to Senegal and other Sahelian countries. By the end of the 1970s, Senegal was receiving approximately $30 million a year in U.S. aid. Senegal has expanded its ties with the United States in other areas. During the mid-1970s, Citibank opened a large branch office in Dakar and stepped up its financial activities. Senegal's flourishing tourist industry also attracted many Americans; by the beginning of the 1980s, approximately 12,000 U.S. tourists were visiting Senegal each year.

Senegal's ties with the United States have been primarily economic. Senghor's pro-French orientation, Senegal's policy of not taking sides in superpower conflicts, and the willingness of the United States to give France a free hand in francophone West Africa were all factors working against Senegal's developing close political ties with the United States. However, it is possible that the two countries may very well develop closer political ties during the 1980s. With its adamant opposition to any Soviet influence in Africa, the Reagan administration sees Senegal, which has sharply criticized Cuban and Soviet involvement in Angola and Ethiopia, as a friend and potential ally.

In the 1970s, Senegal reinforced its ties with Canada, which has channeled most of its Third World aid toward francophone Africa. During the 1970s, Canadian bilateral aid to Senegal surpassed that of the

United States and was second only to that of France. Canada sent large numbers of French-speaking teachers and technicians and built and staffed the Polytechnical Institute in Thiès. The large Canadian presence in Senegal is one of the products of Senghor's appeal to francophone solidarity.

Senegalese relations with the Soviet Union have had their ups and downs since independence. They were probably at their best during the early 1960s when the Soviet Union was actively courting the newly emerging states of Black Africa. Prime Minister Mamadou Dia received an enthusiastic welcome when he visited Moscow on a state visit in June 1962 and signed an economic and technical assistance agreement with the Soviets. Relations cooled after Dia's fall, particularly when the Soviet press criticized Senghor's theories of *négritude* and African Socialism. Relations improved again during the late 1960s and early 1970s when the Soviet Union provided financial assistance for Senegal's tuna fleet and scholarships for Senegalese students to study in the Soviet Union. During this period, Senegal established formal relationships with East Germany and other Eastern European nations. Although Senegal may be moving somewhat closer to the United States, it is unlikely that the country will abandon its policy of nonalignment and openly take the side of the United States in the Cold War between the two superpowers.

NOTES

1. The only major work published in English on Senegalese foreign policy is W.A.E. Skurnik, *The Foreign Policy of Senegal* (Evanston, Ill.: Northwestern University Press, 1972). Unfortunately, this work covers only the first decade of independence and is already dated. Much of the analysis and material in this chapter was culled from French-language periodicals and the Senegalese press. For one of the most thorough analyses of Senegalese foreign policy up through 1978, see Pierre Biarnès, "La diplomatie sénégalaise," [Senegalese diplomacy], *Revue Française d'Etudes Politiques Africaines*, No. 149 (May 1978):62–78.

2. By 1980 Senegal had fifty-two missions abroad and nearly sixty foreign embassies and consulates operating in Dakar. During the 1970s, Senegal's budget for foreign affairs expanded dramatically from little more than 1 billion francs CFA at the beginning of the decade to more than 7 billion francs CFA by 1980. During the latter half of 1980 Senegal closed twenty-three of its overseas missions as part of a broad national austerity program to cut back government spending. Thus far, these measures do not seem to have restrained Senegal's activism on the international scene.

3. Senegalese foreign policy during the Senghor era largely reflected the personality and philosophy of Senghor. For a detailed analysis of the impact of

Senghor's thinking on foreign policy see Skurnik, *Foreign Policy of Senegal*, pp. 184–211 and 275–284.

4. For example, see Jean-Pierre N'Diaye, *La jeunesse africaine face à l'imperialisme* [African youth confronting imperialism] (Paris: François Maspero, 1971).

5. For example, see Senghor's speech at the July 1980 PS National Council denouncing criticisms of Senegalese economic policy appearing in the French press (*Le Soleil*, July 21, 1980).

6. For a detailed description of Gaullist foreign policy and attitudes toward Africa, see Dorothy S. White, *Black Africa and De Gaulle: From the French Empire to Independence* (University Park: Pennsylvania State University Press, 1979).

7. Plans to promote the *trilogue* on a more formal basis were announced at the May 1980 Franco-African summit held in Nice. For more details, see the *New York Times*, May 11, 1980.

8. *Le Soleil*, July 19–20, 1980.

9. Cartierism was the name given to a movement begun in France during the late 1950s to reduce the amount of aid going to France's overseas colonies in order to have more capital available to invest in the metropole. French journalist Raymond Cartier launched the movement with a series of articles appearing in *Paris Match* in August 1956 arguing that the colonies did not pay. After independence Cartier continued his attacks on French aid to francophone Africa, insisting that the money would be better spent in underdeveloped areas of France.

10. For a detailed analysis of the French presence in Senegal, see Rita Cruise O'Brien, *White Society in Black Africa: The French of Senegal* (Evanston, Ill.: Northwestern University Press, 1972).

11. *Marchés Tropicaux*, November 2, 1979.

12. For background to some of the issues raised here, see Alfred G. Gerteiny, *Mauritania* (London: Pall Mall Press, 1967).

13. *Gambia Times*, No. 381 (January 12, 1981).

14. For more on this point, see P-Kiven Tunteng, "External Influences and Subimperialism in Francophone West Africa," in Peter C. W. Gutkind and Immanuel Wallerstein, eds., *The Political Economy of Contemporary Africa* (Beverly Hills, Calif.: Sage Publications, 1976), pp. 212–231.

15. For more background on the story of the Lebanese in West Africa, see R. Bayly Winder, "The Lebanese in West Africa," *Comparative Studies in Society and History* 4, 3 (April 1962):296–333.

16. Club du Sahel/CILSS, *Official Development Assistance to CILSS Member Countries from 1975 to 1979*, Vol. I (Paris: Club du Sahel, 1980), pp. 272–296.

17. See *Marchés Tropicaux*, May 5, 1975, for a brief summary of the evolution of Senegalese-Iranian economic cooperation.

5

Culture and Society

Senegalese culture and society are in flux. Senegal is rapidly becoming urbanized; by the year 2000, more than 40 percent of Senegal's population will be living in towns. Economic stagnation in rural Senegal and the attractions of Dakar have accelerated the rural exodus and aggravated the gap between Dakar and the countryside. Senegalese youth are restless and apprehensive about the future. Juvenile delinquency and street crime are on the rise in the capital city. The elders complain about alcoholism, drug abuse, and the degradation of morals. The women's movement has reached Senegal. A Senegalese woman was one of the chief organizers of the 1980 World Conference on the UN Decade for Women held in Copenhagen, Denmark. And in the countryside, Senegalese women are vociferously demanding relief from the tedious chores of hauling wood, drawing water, and pounding millet, which are traditionally reserved for women. Traditional values of solidarity are under severe stress. The crass materialism of the *nouveaux riches* has been duly noted and exposed by critics of the regime and Senegalese filmmakers like Sembène Ousemane.[1]

Despite the strains in Senegal's social fabric, Senegalese culture has been remarkably resilient in adapting to social change. Notwithstanding rapid urbanization and the spread of secular public education, Islam and the Senegalese Muslim brotherhoods are flourishing and more dynamic than ever. In many parts of rural Senegal, Koranic schools are expanding more rapidly than the public schools, while at the University of Dakar students are renouncing Marxism, turning toward Islam, and becoming *talibés* of Senegalese marabouts. At the same time, many Senegalese intellectuals have committed themselves to modernizing the country along Western lines and striving for prominence in inter-African and international cultural circles. Meanwhile popular culture and the arts continue to evolve, absorbing and Africanizing cultural trends and influences emanating from the Islamic world and the West.

SENEGALESE ISLAM AND
THE MUSLIM BROTHERHOODS

Since the implantation of French colonial rule, Islam has made steady progress. At the turn of the century, less than half Senegal's population was Muslim. Today, more than 90 percent of the people embrace Islam. Since independence, Islam has become an ascendant force in Senegalese society, thanks to the Muslim brotherhoods' ability to adapt to changing social conditions, the spread of Koranic primary schools, and Senegal's growing ties with the Islamic world.

During the colonial period, Muslim brotherhoods were the main vehicles for spreading the Sufi form of Islam and organizing the faithful. Today, most Senegalese Muslims are affiliated with one of Senegal's three principal brotherhoods (Mourides, Tijaniyya, and Qadiriyya).[2] Each brotherhood, or *tariqa* ("the Way" in Arabic), is distinguished by slight differences in ritual and codes of conduct.

The Mouride brotherhood is the most tightly organized and influential in Senegal and has well over a million members. The current khalife-general, Abdoul Lahat M'Backé, has strengthened the brotherhood since taking office following the death of his elder brother, Falilou M'Backé, in 1968. By winning the allegiance of Cheikh M'Backé, a long-time rival of the previous khalife-general, he ended a rift in the brotherhood that had lasted since 1945, when Cheikh M'Backé failed to win the succession. Abdoul Lahat reiterated the gospel of work preached by Amadou Bamba, urged the Mouride marabouts to return to the land, and sharply cut the size of the Mouride bureaucracy. To set an example, he established a large experimental farm and tree nursery on his estate at Touba-Belel and has encouraged his disciples to adopt modern agricultural techniques. In recent years, the Mouride brotherhood has maintained its distance from the state and become a forceful advocate for the interests of the Wolof peanut farmers who constitute the core of its following and an effective instrument for articulating peasant grievances vis-à-vis the state bureaucracy in the peanut basin.[3]

Abdoul Lahat's piety, financial probity, and efforts to reform and modernize the brotherhood have enhanced his popularity among the faithful and won much respect from non-Mourides as well. Mouride influence is growing, especially in areas adjacent to Mouride population centers in the peanut basin. Thanks to their ability to provide capital, jobs, and economic security for their members, the Mourides have won many new followers in Senegal's urban areas. Finally, Western-educated Senegalese have become *talibés* of prominent Mouride marabouts in the hope of gaining support to advance their careers.

Table 5.1
Major Senegalese Islamic brotherhoods

Order	Founder	Ethnic Groups	Location
Qadiri	Abu Bounama Kunta (1780-1840)	Wolof, Moor, Mandinka, Fulbe, Sarakollé, Lebu	Cap Vert, Thiès, Casamance, Fleuve
Mouride	Amadou Bamba M'Backé (1850-1927)	Wolof, Serer	Cap Vert, peanut basin
Tijani	Umar Tall (1794-1864)		
Tijani dynasties			
Sy	Malick Sy (1855-1922)	Wolof, Serer	Cap Vert, Thiès, Sine-Saloum
Niasse	Abdoulaye Niasse (1850-1922)	Wolof, Serer	Sine-Saloum
Tall	Seydou Nourou Tall (1879-1980)	Tukulor	Dakar, Fleuve

One of the most visible signs of Mouride preeminence is the huge attendance at the annual Magal, the religious festival held in Touba, the Mouride capital and site of the largest mosque in West Africa, to commemorate the anniversary of Amadou Bamba's return from exile. Each year, hundreds of thousands of Senegalese crowd the roads to make the pilgrimage to Touba. Representatives of the government, other brotherhoods, and the diplomatic community also attend. The Magal usually features a speech by the Senegalese president or prime minister praising the exemplary work of Amadou Bamba and the contribution of the Mourides to the development of the country, which is often followed by a reply by the grand khalife thanking the government for its assistance and reaffirming the brotherhood's loyalty and affection for the president. The language used in the speeches is carefully scrutinized to assess the status of current relationships between the Mourides and the government.

Although the Mourides are the most influential brotherhood in Senegal, there are more Senegalese who consider themselves to be Tijanis. Most Senegalese Tijanis owe their allegiance to one of three prominent maraboutic houses.

The oldest Tijani house in Senegal traces its roots back to Umar Tall, the Tukulor warrior and empire-builder. For many years, the Tall dynasty was headed by Seydou Nourou Tall, a grandson of Umar. The dynasty's main sphere of influence is in the Senegal River valley. Seydou

Figure 5.1. The great mosque at Touba, religious capital of the Mouride brotherhood. (Photo by Michel Renaudeau)

Nourou Tall also had a large following in Saint Louis and Dakar and played an active role in Senegalese colonial, postwar, and postindependence politics until his death in January 1980 at the venerable age of 101. The Tall dynasty's influence was primarily religious and political rather than economic. In general, Tukulor Tijanis do not display the same degree of reverence and blind obedience to their religious leaders as do the Mourides.

The most prominent Tijani house in Senegal is based in Tivaouane and traces its origins to Malick Sy. The current grand khalife is Abdoul Aziz Sy, who has headed the Sy dynasty since the 1950s. The Sy Tijanis tend to place a greater stress on Islamic education than the Mourides. Since independence, they have promoted the rapid spread of Koranic schools in the region of Thiès and have set up Koranic schools for girls, a marked departure from past traditions of reserving education for the boys. In the rural areas, more Tijani children now attend Koranic schools than secular public schools. Like the Mourides, the Sy dynasty has a large following among the Wolof in the peanut basin, concentrated in what used to be the precolonial state of Cayor and in the new pioneer zones to the east originally settled by followers of Malick Sy.

The third major Senegalese Tijani dynasty has its capital in Kaolack and was founded by Abdoulaye Niasse, a marabout of blacksmith origins. Of the three Senegalese Tijani branches, the Niasse dynasty has had the most ties with the broader Muslim world. Ibrahim Niasse, head of the dynasty until his death in 1975, was widely known in the Arab world for his scholarship and had thousands of *talibés* outside Senegal, notably in northern Nigeria. Niasse himself was less friendly towards Senghor and the Senegalese government than were the heads of the other Senegalese brotherhoods and was a strong proponent of closer ties with the Arab world. He was succeeded by his son Abdoulaye Niasse.

The Qadiriyya is the smallest and also the oldest brotherhood in Senegal. Historically, the Qadiriyya order was introduced in Senegal during the eighteenth and early nineteenth centuries by missionaries from the Niger Bend and Mauritania. The Qadiriyya order has its greatest influence in the Dakar-Thiès metropolitan area and in certain areas of the Casamance. It is divided into several subbranches headed by marabouts having their own followings.

Within Cap Vert, the various Muslim brotherhoods compete for influence, prestige, and new members. Neighborhood "revival" meetings are held frequently, featuring some of Senegal's best male and female singers, who chant verses from the Koran, religious poetry, and the praises of Amadou Bamba, Malick Sy, and other venerated Senegalese holy men.

One of the most recent developments in Senegalese Islam has been the phenomenal expansion of Muslim religious and cultural associations in the Cap Vert region and a growing interest in Islamic theology, philosophy, and the Arabic language. The Islamic cultural revival has been encouraged by Arab countries like Saudi Arabia, Kuwait, Iraq, Egypt, and Libya, which have contributed funds to support Islamic institutes and the study of Arabic in the secondary schools. The brotherhoods are also participating in the Islamic revival, as is reflected in plans to establish both a Mouride and a Tijani Islamic university in Senegal.

The growing involvement of Arab countries in Senegal's Islamic affairs is increasingly evident. The Saudis are contributing funds to build a giant mosque in Tivaouane, while President Saddam Hussein of Iraq has given the Niasse family more than half a million dollars to help build a fine new mosque in Kaolack. Libya is financing Ahmed Niasse's movement to establish an Islamic republic, while Egypt provides hundreds of scholarships for Senegalese to study at Al Azar University in Cairo.

With the resurgence of Islam, the political influence of Senegal's Christian community, which now accounts for less than 5 percent of the population, is clearly on the decline. Many formerly Christian Serer and Diola are changing their names and converting to Islam, particularly in the rural areas. Nearly all Senegal's Christians are Catholics, and two-thirds live in towns. As a group, they have been more exposed to

Western-style education and values than the Muslims. Thanks to mission schools, literacy rates in predominantly Catholic areas of rural Senegal are much higher than in the Muslim areas. In the past, relationships between Senegal's Muslim and Catholic communities have been very good, characterized by mutual tolerance and respect for each other's religion. However, with the departure of Senghor, a Roman Catholic, from the presidency and the rise of fringe Islamic groups calling for the establishment of an Islamic republic, many Christians are becoming more apprehensive about their future. Hence, it is not surprising that the Christian community staunchly supports the survival of Senegal as a secular republic in which all religions will be given equal status.[4]

THE SENEGALESE INTELLIGENTSIA

It is rather remarkable that a small country like Senegal, where most of the population is still illiterate, has been able to produce a relatively large number of scholars, diplomats, writers, filmmakers, and artists who have attained an international reputation for their intellectual and artistic prowess. It would be a mistake to regard the emergence of a Senegalese intelligentsia solely as a by-product of French colonial rule and exposure to Western education. Senegal had its own intelligentsia before colonial rule. The Muslim clerics and holy men who spread Islam also produced treatises on the Koran, Islamic law, and Arabic grammar, as well as religious poetry and philosophy. The reputations of Umar Tall, Malick Sy, and Amadou Bamba were enhanced by their learning and the beauty of their religious poetry. Many of Senegal's leading contemporary intellectuals have come from prominent maraboutic families or began their formal education at Koranic schools.[5]

Politics and culture go hand in hand in Senegal. Senegalese take great pride in their countrymen's intellectual achievements and ability to earn advanced academic degrees. Lamine Guèye's political career received an important boost when he became French West Africa's first Black African lawyer in the early 1920s. Léopold Sédar Senghor also gained much political mileage from the fact that he was the first Black African to pass the difficult French *aggrégation* examination required for teaching in French *lycées*. Given this esteem for culture, it is not surprising that so many of Senegal's leading political personalities are also noted authors, scholars, and men of letters.

Senghor is, of course, the most renowned of Senegal's intellectuals.[6] A product of Catholic mission school education, Senghor went to Paris to continue his studies in the late 1920s. During the 1930s, with Aimé Césaire, he was one of the founders of the *négritude* movement, which revolted against French cultural assimilation and the denigration of traditional African culture. Senghor rejected the premise of African cultural inferiority and extolled the communitarian values and emotional sensibility of Black Africans. Later, he went on to develop a philosophy that stressed the complementarity of different civilizations and the march of humanity toward a "universal civilization." His doctrine of African Socialism, the official ideology of the regime since independence, reflects an effort to blend African communitarian values with modern European socialist thought. As a poet, man of letters, and accomplished linguist, with mastery of Greek, Latin, and several modern European and African languages, Senghor has set a high cultural standard for other Senegalese intellectuals to follow. His poetry[7] written in French has won him many prizes and honors in France, and some literary critics consider him to be one of the most distinguished contemporary poets in the French language. As president, Senghor insisted that Senegal play a leading cultural role in Africa and took great pride in the fact that nearly one-third of the national budget was allocated to education and cultural activities. Even Senegalese who do not share Senghor's views on *négritude* and African Socialism, and his personal preference for French over the national languages, take some pride in Senghor's artistic accomplishments and grudgingly admit that he has done much to enhance the international reputation of Senegalese intellectuals.

Although many young Senegalese in the intelligentsia model themselves on Senghor, Senegalese intellectuals are far from being a homogeneous group. Take, for example, the case of Cheikh Anta Diop, a noted Egyptologist, historian, and opposition leader. Like Senghor, Diop has also earned several advanced academic degrees in French universities. However, unlike Senghor, Diop is an ardent cultural nationalist, advocate of Black African political unity, and Senegalese traditionalist. Through linguistic analysis, Diop has attempted to demonstrate that West Africa was settled as a result of large-scale migratory movements originating in Egypt.[8] As a cultural nationalist, he has called for the adoption of Wolof as Senegal's national language and insisted that African languages are by no means inferior to European languages, as Senghor often implies, in their ability to transmit modern scientific concepts and literary forms of expression. To prove his point, Diop has published scientific articles in Wolof and translated excerpts from European literary masterpieces into Wolof. Diop himself is Wolof and comes from a prominent maraboutic family with close ties to the Mouride brotherhood.

Another example of the diversity and dynamism of Senegalese intellectuals is Ousemane Sembène, author and filmmaker. Unlike Senghor or Cheikh Anta Diop, who take pride in their academic accomplishments, Sembène is a self-educated man who never obtained his primary school diploma—he was expelled for hitting a French teacher who tried to force him to sing French patriotic songs. Barred from public schools, Sembène became an apprentice mechanic and joined the French army during World War II. After the war, he took part in the 1947–1948 Dakar-Niger strike, which became the subject of one of his best-known novels, *God's Bits of Wood*. During the 1950s, he was a dock worker in Marseilles, where he first became exposed to literature, Marxism, and the French Communist party. There he wrote his first novel, *Le Dockeur Noir* [Black dockworker]. Sembène went on to become a prolific writer of novels and short stories that portray the conflict between traditional and modern values, the evils of colonial and neocolonial society, and the struggle of individuals and the masses for freedom and justice. Sembène is a populist, nationalist, and social realist who sees his art as a tool for fighting man's exploitation of man. Rather than attempting to perfect his French, Sembène has tried to "Africanize" his writing by deliberately maintaining Wolof syntax and violating French grammatical rules. He turned to filmmaking in the 1960s in order to reach the African masses, who did not have access to his novels and short stories. His films, which usually deal with themes familiar to Senegalese audiences, have won Sembène much international acclaim. Through films such as *Mandabi, Xaala,* and *Ceddo,* Sembène has provided a potent critique of colonialism, Senegalese society, and the corruption of Senegal's *nouveau riche* bourgeoisie.

A hot topic of debate among Senegalese intellectuals has been the relative importance of French and other European languages vis-à-vis Wolof and other indigenous African languages in the educational system and cultural life of the nation. Although French is the official national language and the language in which all official government business is carried out, only 15 percent of the population can speak or write in French. Senghor and most of the intellectuals in his circle maintained that French should remain the principal language of instruction in the public schools.

Many intellectuals, particularly those in the opposition, have insisted that a foreign language should not be the nation's official language. Moreover, they argue that the priority given to a French-style education has contributed to a sharp social and cultural gap between the Senegalese elite and the masses. Some have argued that Wolof, which is Senegal's lingua franca and understood by nearly 80 percent of the population, should replace French as the official national language. Others have argued that primary school instruction, at least, should be given in one of Senegal's six national languages—Wolof, Pular, Serer, Diola, Mandinka, or Sarakollé, and that the government should step up its program to promote functional literacy in the national languages.

While Senghor headed the Senegalese government, he did little to promote adult literacy in the national languages or even adult literacy in French, preferring that Senegalese pass through the traditional French-style school system and curriculum. He also angered many Senegalese nationalists by assigning the responsibility for developing a grammar for Senegal's national languages to the Centre de Linguistique Appliquée de Dakar (Applied Linguistics Center of Dakar – CLAD), which was run by French scholars. Some of the spelling rules and transcriptions elaborated by CLAD for Wolof during the early 1970s were contested by Senegalese linguists and scholars. The linguistic dispute soon turned into a burning political issue pitting the government against Senegalese nationalists who refused to accept the official orthography. For example, the government stopped Cheikh Anta Diop from publishing an opposition newspaper because he refused to change its Wolof title *Siggi* to conform to the official orthography. In another instance, the film *Ceddo* was banned in Senegal because Sembène would not change the spelling of the title to *Cedo*. Of course, the linguistic dispute was more than just an academic issue; it also reflected sharp political differences between the pro-French Senghor and Senegalese nationalists who saw the French-inspired official orthography as still another manifestation of neocolonialism. Shortly after Senghor retired from the presidency, the new Senegalese government promised to do more to promote Senegal's national languages.

POPULAR CULTURE AND THE ARTS

Senegal's popular culture is rich and vibrant, covering a wide range and blend of traditional African, Islamic, and European values and activities. Like the Americans, the Senegalese are a nation of joiners, especially in the urban areas, where even the humblest Senegalese is a member of some organization. Voluntary associations abound. There are modern, European-style middle-class organizations like the Croix Rouge (Red Cross) and the Soroptimist clubs, Islamic study groups and neighborhood associations grouping together members of the same brotherhood, traditional mutual aid societies made up of men originating from the same village or locality, associations of traditional notables, sports clubs, and veterans groups. Senegal even has its own consumers' movement, which has recently been organized in most of the country's major towns. Whether traditional or modern, each group has a long list of officers and numerous vice-presidents to provide many of its members with a title.

The Senegalese are enthusiastic sports fans. One of the most popular sports is the traditional Senegalese version of wrestling, or *"la lutte,"* which combines theatrical with wrestling skills and provides marvelous entertainment for the spectators. Championship matches often draw crowds of up to 20,000 people. Professional Senegalese wrestlers usually come from lower-caste backgrounds and serve as champions of their respective ethnic group or region. Much of the excitement takes place before the match actually begins as each wrestler tries to psych the other one out by boasting of his prowess and past deeds. Each wrestler has his own entourage of drummers and praise-singers to build him up and intimidate the opponent. The wrestlers also wear many *gris-gris,* or talismans, to give them extra strength and protection. Prominent politicians often attend the matches to be seen and to demonstrate their own high status by sitting in the best seats and freely giving out money to well-wishers and to wrestlers under their patronage.

Soccer, introduced by the French around World War I, is the most popular modern sport in Senegal, particularly among urban youth. On weekends, the soccer stadiums are generally filled to capacity despite the relatively high cost of admission. Senegal has the equivalent of a soccer major league where teams representing different regions in the country play regular schedules and vie for the national championship. The soccer matches often bring out latent regional rivalries and conflicts among the fans. Newcomers to Dakar often root against Cap Vert teams. During the 1980 match for the regional championship, a riot broke out after a questionable call by the referee led to the defeat of the Casamance team by Jeanne d'Arc, a Cap Vert team. The rioting sparked a major shake-up of the national soccer federation by the authorities, who wished to reassure the Casamançais that their teams would be treated more fairly in the future.

The *griots* are the main repositories of traditional Senegalese culture. The majority of *griots* over the age of forty are illiterate and attended neither European nor Koranic schools. The *griot* prepares for his profession as oral historian and musician by doing practical exercises to develop his memory, by learning the genealogies and histories of the great families, and by learning to compose songs and play traditional musical instruments.[9] *Griots* traditionally lived off the generosity of the kings and nobles whom they served. One can still find Senegalese families, particularly among the Tukulor nobility, who have retained their family *griots* and continue to support them financially. The *griots* have kept alive the traditional folk wisdom, which they transmit in the form of stories and proverbs that provide moral lessons and truths for the listener to ponder.[10] In the countryside, storytelling remains one of the most popular forms of recreation in the evening.

Some talented *griots* today earn an excellent living as publicists for political parties and prominent politicians. These *griots* compose and sing songs praising the merits of their patrons or ridiculing their rivals. They are an important part of every major political rally. Other *griots* have learned how to play modern musical instruments like the electric guitar and to manage complicated electronic sound equipment. Many have organized their own bands, which play an eclectic blend of traditional African music combined with modern Black American–style jazz and rhythm and blues. Some bands even have their own female vocalists.

The government has encouraged the preservation of traditional Senegalese music and dance by establishing a national Senegalese ballet company and organizing regional dance troupes and competitions. The Senegalese national ballet company has traveled abroad frequently and enjoyed much praise from Western critics—although some purists argue that the original dances are often jazzed up or in some cases toned down to please European audiences. Performing traditional dances is still one of the most popular forms of recreation in the rural areas, and children learn to dance almost as soon as they learn to walk.

The radio has become perhaps the most important modern medium for transmitting popular culture. The Senegalese national broadcasting system has two main stations, one geared to an urban, Western-educated audience fluent in French, the other aimed at the masses and broadcast in Wolof and other Senegalese languages. The latter tends to play traditional African and Islamic melodies, sermons and commentaries on the Koran by prominent religious personalities, and detailed reports of local news events. Although Senegal has television, it is geared primarily to the educated Senegalese elite and city dwellers who can afford to buy a set. The main programming is in French and consists of a heavy dose of French films, plays, and news programs and rebroadcasts of European soccer matches and variety shows. The Senegalese television network also provides literacy programs in the national languages, plays and variety shows in Wolof, and extensive coverage of Senegalese political events from a progovernment perspective.

Although French is the official language of the country and the main language of instruction in the schools, it has not become an integral part of popular culture. Even the most educated Senegalese are far from becoming "Black Frenchmen" culturally. Most Senegalese prefer to speak their first language at home and among friends. A CLAD-sponsored survey of Senegalese schoolchildren found that less than 1 percent of Senegalese households used French as their primary language. The same survey also found that most urban schoolchildren, particularly the younger ones, spoke Wolof. The children of the Serer, Tukulor, Diola, and Fulbe who settled in Dakar and other big towns thus communicate with each other in Wolof, which they usually speak better than their own language. The Dakar Wolof dialect, which absorbs or Africanizes many French words and European concepts into its vocabulary, is fast becoming Senegal's unofficial national language.

The rise of an urban Dakar-Wolof mass culture has also been accompanied recently by a resurgence in Islamic piety, which has led to a greater popular interest in learning Muslim law and Arabic. One element in the Islamic revival is the growing criticism of the decline of traditional values among Senegal's urban youth, reflected in sharp attacks on alcoholism, sexual promiscuity, and lack of respect for parental authority. In the future it is likely that one will see more clashes at the mass level between the exuberant modern urban Wolof culture and the conservative and more austere Islamic culture.

INTERETHNIC RELATIONSHIPS

As a society, Senegal has been remarkably free of the racial and ethnic strife that has plagued many other African nations. Race has not been a major issue in Senegalese politics since the early colonial period. After independence, French and Lebanese residents, if they wished, had the option of adopting Senegalese citizenship. Senegal has also been tolerant of non-Senegalese Africans coming to live and work in the country. Despite rising unemployment and growing economic problems, there have been no mass expulsions of "stranger" populations in Senegal similar to the expulsion of the Dahomeans from Niger in the early 1960s or that of the Nigerians from Ghana in the late 1960s.

Senegal's national unity is unlikely to be threatened by interethnic strife. Its precolonial political traditions and long colonial history have helped forge a strong sense of Senegalese national identity among the majority of the people. Even the peasants in the countryside tend to regard their Senegalese identity as more important than their ethnic identity. This tendency is much more pronounced among the young. A poll of peasant attitudes taken in the late 1960s showed that 80 percent of those surveyed under the age of thirty-five stressed their Senegalese national identity over that of their ethnic group.[11]

The Wolof, who account for 35 to 40 percent of Senegal's total population are the largest and most influential ethnic group in the country[12] and have the most highly developed sense of Senegalese nationality. As we have seen, their language and culture, particularly in the urban areas, is rapidly becoming a national one that transcends Wolof ethnicity. The Wolof have been very active in Senegalese politics and hold a disproportionate share of cabinet posts and seats in the National Assembly. The Wolof are highly urbanized and tend to believe that they are more advanced than other Senegalese ethnic groups. Other ethnic groups in Senegal admire them for their initiative and ability to adapt.

The Wolof have few restrictions on intermarriage with other ethnic groups.

The Serer, who once had the reputation of being staunch traditionalists who kept to themselves, have been undergoing rapid Islamization and Wolofization since independence. Thus, Serer migrating to Dakar are assimilating into the dominant Wolof urban culture while many rural Serer in the peanut region have also been adopting Wolof lifestyles and agricultural techniques after converting to Islam and joining predominantly Wolof brotherhoods. The Serer have a reputation for being a hard-working and industrious people, particularly skilled in traditional farming methods.

The Lebu, a small but influential people closely related to the Serer, have long been Wolofized. The Lebu are concentrated almost exclusively in the Cap Vert region. Lebu notables own a good deal of valuable real estate in Dakar and Rufisque, and Lebu fishermen dominate Senegal's fishing industry. Although the Wolof-speaking Lebu retain their own distinct ethnic identity, they tend to identify themselves primarily as Senegalese. Together, the Wolof, Serer, and Lebu constitute more than half of Senegal's total population.

The greatest potential for interethnic conflict within Senegal is likely to come from Senegal's other ethnic groups, which are concentrated in the so-called peripheral regions. Even here, the source of conflict is not so much ethnicity as regionalism and religion. Although the Tukulor have a strong sense of ethnic identity, they also tend to regard themselves as Senegalese. They are particularly critical of the discrimination practiced against the Tukulor minority in Mauritania; but they also resent what they feel to be the discrimination against their region practiced by both the colonial regime and, more recently, the national government. Ironically, the government's present plans to transform the Fleuve region through massive dam and irrigation projects may exacerbate tensions by upsetting the traditional land tenure system and bringing in non-Tukulor populations to work the land. Reputed to be the most pious of Senegal's ethnic groups, the Tukulor do not look favorably upon the great and growing influence exercised by the predominantly Wolof Muslim brotherhoods in the country's political and religious life. Tukulor traditionalists deplore the Wolofization process going on among Tukulor living in Dakar and other major urban areas, yet the Tukulor still tend to resist Wolofization more than other Senegalese ethnic groups.

Another source of tension and interethnic conflict may come from the Casamance, where the Diola, Mandinka, and other smaller ethnic groups have been developing a strong regional Casamançais identity. Less traditionalist and more individualistic than the Tukulor, the

Casamançais have not reacted strongly against the Wolofization process taking place in Ziguinchor and among Casamançais living in Cap Vert. On the other hand, they feel resentment against what they consider to be discrimination against the Casamance and against Casamançais in the urban areas.

Senegal's non-African population has dropped sharply since independence, from 60,000 in 1960 to 30,000 by 1975. More than 90 percent of Senegal's non-African population, mostly French and Lebanese, live in Cap Vert. Although there have been occasional outbursts of hostility against the French since independence, as was the case during the May-June 1968 crisis, these were motivated largely by nationalist rather than racialist sentiments. The decline of the French population; the departure of thousands of French skilled workers and mechanics in the private sector; and the Africanization of the administration, Chamber of Commerce, and teaching corps have contributed to a lessening of racial tensions between the Senegalese and the French community.

The Lebanese community, which now numbers about 15,000, continues to play an important role in the Senegalese economy. Unlike the French, most of the Lebanese who came to Senegal learned Wolof and other Senegalese languages and tried to develop friendly ties with prominent Senegalese political and religious personalities, to whom they looked for protection. Since independence, the Senegalese government has refrained from launching anti-Lebanese campaigns or nationalizing Lebanese firms despite complaints from Senegalese businessmen who see the Lebanese as blocking their entry into many areas of business. Although the majority of Lebanese in Senegal have taken Senegalese citizenship, they nevertheless remain a vulnerable group because they are still regarded as foreigners by most Senegalese and frequently criticized by Senegalese nationalists.

Senegal has been generous in its treatment of its approximately 300,000 non-Senegalese Africans. Tens of thousands of Guineans fleeing from Sékou Touré's Guinea have flocked to Senegal, settling in Dakar and the rural areas near the Senegalese-Guinean border. Senegal has also permitted francophone African cadres from Mali, Dahomey, and other West African countries to hold jobs in both government and the private sector. Of all the non-Senegalese Africans, the Moors from Mauritania are the most integrated into the Senegalese economy and society. Moor shopkeepers can be found in nearly every urban neighborhood in the Dakar-Thiès metropolitan areas. Although some Moors hold Senegalese citizenship, relations between the Moors and other Senegalese ethnic groups are sometimes tense. The lighter-skinned Moors often look down upon the Senegalese; many Senegalese do not like doing business with the Moors, who are often depicted as tight-fisted and greedy merchants.

Relations among different Senegalese groups are generally good, even though there is some ethnic rivalry between the Wolof and the Tukulor and between older Dakar residents and newcomers. There is little racial antagonism against Senegal's Afro-European *métis* population, who despite the relative decline of their community still play a vital role in Senegal's political, economic, and cultural life. For many years Jean Diallo, an Afro-European and former French army officer, headed the Senegalese army, and André Guillabert, another Afro-European, has served as ambassador to France and held several major cabinet posts during a long and distinguished political career. Although religious affiliation is a more important factor than ethnicity as an organizing principle in Dakar, Senegal does have its own brand of ethnic politics operating at both the national and local levels. The national government thus attempts to give representation to the major ethnic groups in the country, and government ministers tend to choose their closest collaborators from their own ethnic groups. On the other hand, the government has outlawed ethnic political associations and parties, and the PS has discouraged the establishment of ethnic caucuses within local party units.

WOMEN

One of the most significant developments in Senegalese society since independence has been the change in the role and status of women. Greater participation by women in Senegalese politics and rural development programs has been promoted by greater access to education and government policies instituted since the mid-1970s. Senegalese women now have greater expectations for a larger voice in society, especially in the urban areas.

Throughout most of the colonial period, Senegalese women were confined largely to traditional roles and had little access to formal education. As late as 1965, fewer than 1 percent of Senegalese women could speak or write in French. During the colonial period, Muslim girls rarely went to public school and few attended school as frequently as boys. However, since independence, there has been a sharp rise in the number and percentage of Senegalese girls going to school. In 1961 the ratio of boys to girls attending primary school was more than 2 to 1; by 1976 that ratio had narrowed to less than 3 to 2 and the number of girls in school had more than tripled, from 41,000 to 131,000.[13] Moreover, the number and percentage of Muslim girls attending Koranic school also rose dramatically during the 1970s and early 1980s.

Before 1946 Senegalese women, even residents of the four communes, were not allowed to vote. In the postwar period, although they had been given the suffrage and were active in urban Senegalese politics, Senegalese women held no major political office. Women were absent

Figure 5.2. Urban Koranic school. (Photo by Michel Renaudeau)

from the National Assembly until 1963, when Caroline Diop became Senegal's first woman deputy. Fifteen years later, however, in the 1978 national legislative elections, all three contending parties had several women candidates on their electoral lists. Following the elections, Caroline Diop and Maimouna Kane became the first women to attain ministerial rank in a Senegalese government. Both women have played a highly visible role in national and international women's politics and have used their offices to vigorously promote the status of women. Despite recent gains made by Senegalese women, Senegalese men will continue to dominate Senegalese politics in the years to come, especially in the rural areas where there are fewer educated women and where families tend to vote as a block, following the lead of the male family leader.

Senegal's educated women in recent years have also begun to make their mark on the intellectual and cultural life of the nation. Women constitute more than one-third of the University of Dakar's total enrollment. Senegal has produced distinguished women writers like Mariama Ba and Aminata Sow Fall, whose novels have won prizes in Senegal and in Europe.[14] A small number of Senegalese women professors now teach at the University of Dakar, conduct research at the prestigious Institut Fondamental d'Afrique Noire (Basic Research Institute of Black Africa—IFAN), and present papers at international conferences. A Senegalese woman heads the Institute for Food Technology, another edits *Famille et Développement*, a Dakar-based magazine widely read throughout francophone Africa.

Change has proceeded more rapidly in Dakar, where women have been entering the labor market as secretaries, typists, sales clerks, maids, and unskilled workers in textile mills and tuna-canning factories.[15] Four thousand women worked as farm laborers for BUD-Sénégal before its collapse in late 1979. Morals and mores are also evolving more rapidly in the urban areas, where the elders complain about a shocking rise in teenage sexual promiscuity and many Senegalese middle-class women are beginning to advocate family planning. Senegal's 1972 Family Code, which provides greater legal protection and rights for women, has also had a much greater impact in the towns than in the countryside.

Senegal was one of the first African countries to establish a rural development agency—Animation Feminine—designed specifically to organize village women to improve the quality of family and village life and to involve them more actively in the development process. Since the late 1970s, the government has stepped up its efforts to deliver more services to rural women. For example, women have welcomed the mechanical millet mills distributed with great fanfare by women ministers on their visits to the interior. There are also signs that women are participating more in rural political and economic institutions. Some rural councils have women representatives, and in many areas women are putting pressure on the rural councils to buy millet mills and carts to make the women's traditional tasks of pounding millet and gathering wood easier. Rural women are also beginning to participate more in adult literacy programs and agricultural extension programs set up by the government's technical services.

Access to formal education and rural animation programs is steadily transforming the traditional attitudes of rural women, while the predominantly male exodus from the rural areas is destabilizing family and village structures and putting more of a burden on the women left behind. Despite changes in the countryside, there is still a wide and even growing social and cultural gap between the better-educated and more sophisticated women of Dakar and their sisters in the countryside that reflects the general social and cultural gap between the capital and the interior.

YOUTH

Senegal's national leaders have often insisted that the country's future lies with the youth. Like most developing nations, Senegal has a young population, with more than 52 percent of its population under the age cf twenty. And like youth in many developing countries, Senegalese youth are embracing new values and becoming increasingly restless about their future.

The need to provide jobs and a productive place in society for the rising tide of Senegalese youth entering the job market each year has become one of the most difficult tasks facing the country, one that affects rural as well as urban youth. Each year more than 20,000 young Senegalese enter the urban labor market. The great majority are school-leavers with limited modern skills and relatively high expectations as to future living standards. Some are illiterate peasants seeking temporary or permanent jobs in the towns in an effort to escape extremely low living standards in the countryside. Finally, there are the better-educated secondary school and university graduates seeking good jobs in government or the private sector. Senegal's stagnant economy has not been able to provide adequate employment opportunities for urban youth, leading to steadily rising levels of unemployment.

During the first two decades of independence, Africanization permitted the government to find employment for most of Senegal's secondary school and university graduates. However, the future for many members of this group looks less promising. The number of secondary school students more than doubled, from 38,000 in 1968 to nearly 80,000 by 1980, while the number of Senegalese students at the University of Dakar increased from 1,250 to nearly 10,000 during the same period.[16] Although students constitute a privileged group within Senegalese society, student unrest may eventually pose a serious threat to the stability of the regime, especially if large numbers of students fail to find work in the government or private sector.

The less educated urban youth are also restless. Juvenile delinquency and street crime have become a major concern in recent years, and there are some parts of Dakar where it is no longer safe to walk the streets at night. To correct the situation, religious leaders are conducting campaigns attacking the degradation of morals and the decline of traditional values and morality. Secular opposition intellectuals blame government corruption and neocolonial economic policies for fostering greed and unemployment, and they appeal to Senegal's urban youth to reject the regime. For its part, the government has used patronage and the Youth and Sports Ministry to provide jobs and athletic facilities for Senegalese urban youth.

Although their lifestyles and educational levels are markedly different, Senegal's rural youth share many similar kinds of concerns. In many densely populated areas of rural Senegal, there is no longer sufficient land available to support young unmarried males, who are obliged to work for their parents, migrate to the new pioneer zones, or go to the towns to look for jobs. Even in areas where there is sufficient land to cultivate, the unremunerative nature of Senegalese agriculture has led many rural Senegalese, especially those who have been to school, to seek their fortune in the towns. During the dry season, hundreds of Senegalese villages are literally emptied of their young males, who do not return until the rains come to inaugurate the next planting season. The lack of opportunities to earn money at home and the difficulty of finding employment in the towns have led many young Senegalese to go abroad. There are an estimated 50,000 Senegalese now working in France as janitors, street-cleaners, and unskilled laborers. Most are Tukulor or Sarakollé from the Senegal River valley.[17] Many learn how to read and write in France and become radicalized. Their earnings help support the families they leave behind. When they return, they often bring with them new ideas and values and a willingness to invest in modern agricultural techniques.

In addition to its high degree of mobility, Senegalese rural youth are also less attached to traditional values than their elders, and more individualistic. They have fewer caste biases and are more willing to marry outside their ethnic groups. Lower-caste youth are also less willing to accept orders from the traditional nobility. One of the major concerns of Senegalese youth is the high cost of the bride-price, which prevents many men from getting married before their mid-thirties. Like their urban brothers, rural youth enthusiastically support government efforts to put an official ceiling on the bride-price.

In the past, the government has given most of its attention to the problems of urban youth. However, in recent years, it has stepped up its efforts to provide more incentives for rural youth to stay in the countryside in order to stem the rural exodus and revitalize Senegalese agriculture. Thus, the government has set up special training programs for young artisans, peasants, and herders to enable them to earn a better living; established youth villages and pioneer settlements that provide young peasants with land and farming implements; and set up more rural youth centers and athletic facilities.

Given Senegal's current economic difficulties, the country will be hard pressed to find sufficient employment opportunities for its youth in the near future. If the government does not stem the rising tide of urban youth unemployment or improve the living standards of young peasants, the social climate, already under duress, is likely to deteriorate still further and pose a serious threat to the country's stability.

NOTES

1. See, for example, Sembène's film *Xaala*, which brilliantly satirizes the pretensions of Senegal's nouveaux riches. The film depicts the fall of a pompous middle-aged Senegalese businessman who is unable to fulfill his marital obliga-

tions after taking a young woman as a third wife because of a *xaala*, or curse, placed on him to render him impotent.

2. According to official Senegalese statistics, the Tijaniyya brotherhood is the largest in Senegal, with 51.5 percent of the population identifying themselves as Tijanis in 1970. However, the Tijaniyya brotherhood is subdivided into several different branches or houses, none of which is as large as the Mouride brotherhood, which encompassed 29 percent of the population in 1970. Only 13.5 percent of the population were affiliated with the Qadiriyya brotherhood in 1970. For more details on the size, composition, and geographical concentration of the different Senegalese brotherhoods, see Senegal, Republic of, *Atlas national du Sénégal* (Paris: Institut de Géographie National, 1977), pp. 70–72.

3. See Donal B. Cruise O'Brien, "Ruling Class and Peasantry in Senegal, 1960–1976" in Rita Cruise O'Brien, ed., *The Political Economy of Underdevelopment: Dependence in Senegal* (Beverly Hills, Calif.: Sage Publications, 1979), pp. 220–226.

4. See, for example, the account of a debate on this theme sponsored by Club Nation et Développement appearing in *Le Soleil,* January 14, 1980.

5. For a greater understanding of the impact of Koranic education upon the formation of Senegalese Muslim intellectuals, see Cheikh Hamidou Kane's novel *Ambiguous Adventure* (New York: Collier Books, 1969).

6. For two major works in English on Senghor's intellectual development and thought, see Jacques Louis Hymans, *Léopold Sédar Senghor: An Intellectual Biography* (Edinburgh: Edinburgh University Press, 1971); and Irving Leonard Markovitz, *Léopold Sédar Senghor and the Politics of Negritude* (New York: Atheneum, 1969).

7. See, for example, *Ethiopiques* (Paris: Editions du Seuil, 1956); and *Nocturnes* (Paris: Editions du Seuil, 1961).

8. See *Nations nègres et culture* [Black nations and culture] (Paris: Présence Africaine, 1955); *L'unité culturelle de l'Afrique noire* [The cultural unity of Black Africa] (Paris: Présence Africaine, 1959); and *L'Afrique noire précoloniale* [Precolonial Black Africa] (Paris: Présence Africaine, 1960).

9. For a fascinating discussion of the *griot*'s training, see Assane Sylla, *La philosophie morale des Wolof* [The moral philosophy of the Wolof] (Dakar: Sankoré, 1978), pp. 121–123.

10. For excellent examples of Senegalese folk tales, see Birago Diop, *Les contes d'Amadou-Koumba* [Tales of Amadou-Koumba] (Paris: Présence Africaine, 1961).

11. See Pierre Fougeyrollas, *Où va le Sénégal?: Analyse spectrale d'une nation africaine* [Where is Senegal going? A spectrum analysis of an African nation] (Paris: Editions Anthropos, 1970), pp. 51–54.

12. There are no accurate figures concerning the ethnic composition of Senegal's population. For example, demographic studies done in the early 1960s indicated that less than 36 percent of the population were Wolof. The Fifth Senegalese Plan, which was published in 1976, claimed that more than 40 percent of the population were Wolof. With the process of Wolofization taking place in Senegal, these figures cited may well be accurate. However, the Fifth Senegalese Plan also states that the Serer constitute about 19 percent of the

population, as compared with slightly less than 14 percent of the population listed in earlier studies. Such a sharp increase in the percentage of Serer is highly unlikely because the Serer themselves have been undergoing Wolofization more rapidly than any other Senegalese ethnic group.

13. Senegal, Republic of, *Le Sénégal en chiffres, editions 1978* (Dakar: Société Africaine d'Editions, 1979), p. 51.

14. For example, see Mariama Ba, *Une si longue lettre* [A very long letter] (Dakar: Nouvelles Editions Africaines, 1980); and Aminata Sow Fall, *La grève des Battù* [The strike of the beggars] (Dakar: Nouvelles Editions Africaines, 1980).

15. For a discussion of Senegal's working women, see Francine Kane, "Femmes prolétaires du Sénégal, à la ville et aux champs" [Proletarian women of Senegal in the city and the countryside], *Cahiers d'Etudes Africaines* 17, 65 (1976):77–94.

16. *Le Soleil*, November 3, 1980.

17. For a detailed discussion of why they leave their homes and go to France, see Adrian Adams, *Le long voyage des gens du fleuve Sénégal* [The long journey of the Senegal River people] (Paris: François Maspero, 1977).

6

Toward the Year 2000: Whither Senegal?

On December 4, 1980, *Le Soleil* announced that Léopold Sédar Senghor would retire as president of the republic at the end of the year. Although speculation and rumors concerning the 74-year-old Senghor's impending retirement had been circulating for months, the official announcement nevertheless caught the general public by surprise. This time, the rumors were true.

Senghor departed gracefully, the first African head of state to leave office of his own accord. On January 1, 1981, Abdou Diouf, Senghor's hand-picked successor, was sworn in as Senegal's new president without incident. Diouf pledged to continue the policies of his mentor, but he also hinted that there would be some changes. The Senghor era was over. Henceforth, younger men would assume full responsibility for guiding the nation's destiny on post-Senghorian Senegal's march toward the year 2000.

SENGHOR AND THE MYSTIQUE OF THE YEAR 2000

Economics was not Senghor's forte. When he stepped down from office, the country was on the brink of bankruptcy, its peanut-based economy in shambles. He left the masses with an ailing economy and his successors committed to a hopeful vision of the future incarnated in the Mystique of the Year 2000.

Senghor first launched the Mystique of the Year 2000 in December 1969 in his report to the Seventh UPS National Party Congress.[1] Rather than dwelling on the country's current economic difficulties, Senghor exhorted the party faithful to look to the future. Senghor held out a vision of a modern and prosperous Senegal in the year 2000, a Senegal that by then would have tripled real per capita income and entered the ranks of the world's industrialized nations. For Senghor, the poet-philosopher, the new millenium would be a particularly appropriate time for Senegal to enter a new and higher stage in its national development.

The Mystique of the Year 2000 influenced the Senghor regime's economic thinking throughout the 1970s and led to a major emphasis on large-scale, long-term development projects designed to radically transform Senegal's colonial economic structures and move the locus of the economy away from peanuts. This strategy compelled Senghor and his government to look outside Senegal to obtain the capital and technology needed to implement their ambitious programs. Drought and other economic setbacks prevented the country from making much progress. Real per capita income stagnated or declined rather than rising at the projected 5.5 percent annual rate needed to attain a tripling of per capita income by the end of the century. Grandiose economic schemes failed to materialize or were delayed because of lack of financing. Chronic drought and bureaucratic mismanagement held back agriculture. Growing trade deficits and heavy government borrowing abroad led to an alarming increase in the country's external debt.

Yet, despite the setbacks, the Senghor regime clung steadfastly to its optimism about Senegal's long-range prospects and took pride in its ability to win the confidence of foreign donors and governments. In the future, things would be better. Senegal had oil off the Casamance coast and extensive iron ore deposits that would soon be exploited. Foreign investors would flock to Senegal's tax-free industrial port zone, spurring employment and exports. The construction of dams in the Senegal River basin and the Casamance would increase rural incomes, end the country's food dependency, and provide a margin of security against the effects of drought.

The great gap between Senghor's bright vision of the future and the grim economic realities facing Senegal in the early 1980s can be summed up in a story that was widely circulated shortly before Senghor departed from the presidency. When Senghor laid the cornerstone for the construction of the Diama dam in late 1979, he spoke lyrically of the Senegal River basin's economic potential and the great prosperity that would come to Senegal after the dam was completed. Not everyone shared the president's enthusiasm, particularly in a year in which drought had once again made life very difficult for most of Senegal's rural population. A few months later, Senghor met with Abdoul Lahat M'Backé, the grand khalife of the Mourides, to discuss important matters concerning the country. To reassure the Mouride leader that Senegal's economic woes would pass, Senghor evoked the image of a prosperous Senegal that would easily solve all its food problems by the year 2010, thanks to the dam projects. "That is all well and good," replied the marabout. "But by

Figure 6.1. Harvesting fish along the Senegal River. Much of Senegal's economic future depends upon full utilization of the resources of the Senegal River. (Photo by Julie Stedman)

then, you and I will be long since in our graves. Our peasants are hungry now. What are you going to do for them today?"

SENEGAL'S ECONOMIC FUTURE: PROSPERITY OR DISASTER?

President Diouf assumed office in the midst of Senegal's most severe financial and economic crisis since independence. Two consecutive years of drought had dashed all hopes of a speedy economic recovery. Peanut production had plummeted to 400,000 tons in the 1980-1981 season.[2] At 550,000 tons, millet and sorghum production were well below the record levels obtained two years earlier. And rice production had fallen to 68,000 tons, a far cry from the 220,000 tons originally called for by the end of Senegal's Fifth Plan (1977–1981).

The situation was further aggravated by the lowest level of peanut commercialization since World War II. Just before the 1980 planting season, the government had antagonized large segments of the rural population by holding back on the distribution of seed peanuts until the cooperatives had repaid most of their debts. The late distribution of seed had an adverse effect on peanut production, as peanut farmers devoted more land to food crops. As a result, millet production surpassed peanut production for the first time in nearly forty years. After the harvest, many farmers balked at selling their peanuts to the government for fear that the receipts would be withheld from them to repay old debts. Others retained part of their crop to make sure they would have seed for the next season. The dissolution of ONCAD, although welcomed by the population, had also created some confusion in the traditional peanut trade for the 1980-1981 season. As a result, only 200,000 tons of peanuts were commercialized through official channels. Moreover, Senegal's peanut oil industry could obtain only 100,000 tons for its own use, about one-eighth the amount it needed to run at full capacity. This meant that Senegal had precious little peanut oil to export in 1981 and would lose tens of millions of dollars in foreign exchange and see its trade deficits soar to record heights.

To redress a catastrophic situation, Diouf was obliged to take bold measures to regain the confidence of the rural population and provide sufficient incentives to restore agricultural production.[3] In April 1981, he canceled previous debts for seed and fertilizer and declared a moratorium on the repayment of debts for agricultural equipment until conditions improved. To bolster peanut production, Diouf announced that peanut prices for the 1981-1982 season would be raised from 50 to 70 francs CFA per kilo. The government also increased millet and rice prices by 25 percent. The announcement of higher prices came before the planting season to encourage the rural population to grow more peanuts and food crops.

In addition to the near collapse of the rural economy, Diouf had to contend with a huge foreign debt and pressures placed on his government by the World Bank, IMF, and other donors to clamp down on government spending and accept a wide range of austerity measures that would depress urban living standards and sharply reduce the special benefits previously received by high-ranking civil servants. Until the mid-1980s, Senegal's urban population will have to bear the brunt of the government's austerity programs. They will be paying higher prices for food and other basic commodities that had been subsidized in the past. Their wages will probably not keep up with inflation. To attract foreign investors for Senegal's tax-free industrial export zone, the government will try to hold wages down. With many small and medium-sized Senegalese firms closing down because of the current economic recession and more stringent credit restrictions, urban unemployment will remain high. Public-sector employment will become increasingly hard to find because of freezes in the national budget and the closing down of more parastatal agencies. These hardships will not be readily accepted by the urban masses unless they are satisfied that the Senegalese elite is also accepting its fair share of the sacrifices and renouncing some of its past privileges.

To win support for its austerity programs, the Diouf regime promised to maintain the living standards of the urban poor and to reduce the gap in salaries and benefits between the highest-paid and lowest-paid Senegalese workers. Despite these measures, however, it seems likely that urban unrest will probably rise in the face of mounting inflation and unemployment, which will lead to intense pressure on the Diouf government to back off from its austerity programs.

The regime found itself in a difficult bind. If it retreated from its austerity programs, it would displease the IMF, World Bank, and other Western donors and creditors whose support it needed to keep the economy afloat. The loss of such support would jeopardize the regime's efforts to improve Senegal's precarious financial status and obtain the capital needed to carry out its long-range development programs. On the other hand, if it imposed too many burdens on the urban masses and important segments of the bureaucracy, it would become increasingly unpopular. The political opposition had already attacked the government for accepting the IMF "Diktat" and placing the economy in the hands of international capitalism.[4]

Despite the grim economic realities and prospects for economic disaster looming around the corner, the first year of the post-Senghorian era was marked by tangible signs that some of the *grands projets*[5] formulated during the 1970s were more than just wishful thinking. On March 11, 1981, President Diouf inaugurated the official opening of Dakar-Marine, a $75 million project that modernized and expanded the port of Dakar's ship-repair facilities. In early April he laid the cornerstone for the Industries Chimiques du Sénégal (ICS), which he characterized as Senegal's most important industrial project since independence.[6] ICS was established to create a fertilizer export industry based on Senegal's abundant phosphate reserves. Shareholders in ICS, a model of Third World collaboration, also include Nigeria, the Ivory Coast, the Islamic Development Bank, and private Indian fertilizer companies. ICS was scheduled to begin production in 1984 and eventually to export 25 billion francs CFA worth of fertilizer annually. Optimistic reports were also made concerning the exploitation of Senegal's iron ore reserves, which proved to be larger than anticipated.[7] MIFERSO enlarged its equity capital and made plans to launch the first phase of operations in 1987. The massive project required 200 billion francs CFA and envisaged mining 12 million tons of iron a year and the construction of a new railroad and port to evacuate the iron and ship it abroad.

As for the Diama and Manantali dams, the Organisation de Mise en Valeur du Fleuve Sénégal (Organization for the Development of the Senegal River–OMVS), which had been created in 1972 by Senegal, Mali, and Mauritania, was on the verge of obtaining enough financing to proceed with construction.[8] By the middle of 1981, a consortium of donors led by Saudi Arabia had pledged 90 percent of the credits needed to launch the first phase of the project. But even with both projects under way, no major results could be expected until the 1990s.

Like Senghor, Diouf has counted heavily upon the support of foreign donors to help carry the country through its economic difficulties. Senegalese diplomacy has succeeded remarkably well in obtaining the external resources needed to avert economic disaster and to initiate some of the large-scale development programs designed to make the bright future envisaged in the Mystique of the Year 2000 a reality. But time may be running out. And the donors' patience may be wearing thin. In 1980, Senegal's foreign debt was 203 billion francs CFA and growing, while the cost of servicing the debt had soared to 41 billion francs CFA for the 1980-1981 fiscal year.[9] If this trend continues unchecked, Senegal could lose its credibility with foreign donors and investors. In 1982, the situation looked somewhat better, thanks to a good 1981-1982 peanut crop and promises of more aid from France and the Arab world.

SENEGAL'S POLITICAL FUTURE: STABILITY OR REVOLUTION?

Upon assuming the presidency, Abdou Diouf pledged that his regime would continue the policies of his mentor, Senghor. Diouf promised to preserve Senegal's pluralistic multiparty political system, African Socialism, as the regime's official ideology, and the main lines of Senghorian foreign policy with its stress on Senegal's special relationship with France. To underscore continuity with the Senghor regime, Diouf retained most of the ministers who had served in the previous government and named Habib Thiam, another long-time Senghor protégé, as his prime minister.[10]

Although groomed to succeed Senghor for more than a decade, the new president did not have a reputation as a strong political personality. Instead, he was widely regarded as a modest, if not timid, technocrat who faithfully served Senghor and the state. There were some doubts whether the mild-mannnered Diouf would have the necessary authority, strength, and political skills to lead the country in such difficult times or to control the various factions contending for power within his own party. Once in office, however, Diouf surprised many people by quickly moving to assert his authority and style of political leadership and affirming his independence of Senghor.[11]

In January 1981, President Diouf formally replaced Senghor as secretary-general of the PS. Diouf wisely named several leaders of the "old guard" as deputy secretary-generals. This display of renewed respect for the graybeards of the party, who had seen their power wane with the rise of the younger technocrats, won Diouf their support and warm pledges of loyalty. At the same time, Diouf placed his closest political collaborators in key organizational posts within the PS, thereby ensuring his control over the party apparatus.

The new president also greatly enhanced his personal prestige and established himself as a national leader in his own right after a triumphal visit to Saudi Arabia to attend the Islamic Conference held in Taif in late January 1981.[12] Senegalese television coverage showed Diouf praying in the holy city of Mecca and being graciously received by Saudi leaders as the official spokesman for the views of the Muslim Sahelian francophone nations. When Diouf returned home, he received a hero's welcome from Senegal's Muslims, who were proud to see Senegal recognized as a Muslim nation and led by a Muslim leader, something that had not been possible under the Catholic Senghor. Diouf's announcement that he had obtained a $50 million grant from Saudi Arabia and $40 million from Iraq for the Senegal River basin project as a result of his efforts at the

Figure 6.2. Prime Minister Abdou Diouf with the late King Faisal and other Saudi leaders. With Diouf as president, Senegal has become one of Saudi Arabia's closest African allies. Photo by Michel Renaudeau.

Taif conference bolstered his image even more. Further reinforcement of his international stature as a prominent Muslim leader came with an official state visit to Saudi Arabia in March 1982, when Diouf was received with great warmth by Saudi leaders.

Shortly after taking power, the Diouf government organized the Etats Généraux de l'Enseignement (Estates General of Education) (January 28-31, 1981), a broad forum that brought together representatives of the government, teachers' unions, parents' associations, and other groups concerned with education to discuss the future of Senegal's educational system.[13] The meeting went a long way toward defusing the potentially explosive situation caused by the growing alienation of large numbers of students, teachers, and urban youth during the 1979-1980 school year, which was marked by student strikes and violence, an unsuccessful attempt to strike by SUDES, the radical antigovernment teachers' union, and the government's firing of most of SUDES's leaders from their teaching posts.

Senegal's educational policies under Senghor had been a sore spot for a large segment of the Senegalese intelligentsia, who thought that the Senegalese French-based educational system was poorly adapted to the country's needs and was a form of cultural neocolonialism. The presence of nearly a thousand French teachers in the school system reinforced this impression, as did Senghor's resistance to making the national languages a more important part of the school system. With Senghor gone, Diouf was free to adopt a new direction.

Both the government and SUDES dropped their confrontational stances and sat down together to discuss their respective points of view in a spirit of reconciliation. At the end of the conference, the government committed itself to a major reform of the educational system and co-opted many of the educational policies advocated by SUDES and Senegalese nationalists on the left. Thus, the government promised to institute universal primary school education by 1990, make the curriculum less literary and more practical, accelerate the use of the national languages as a medium of instruction, and sharply reduce the number of foreign teachers serving in the Senegalese school system, with the objective of phasing out all technical assistance personnel within ten years. On the other hand, the government firmly resisted the demands of SUDES for a 50 percent salary increase for schoolteachers, insisting that the government could not afford it and that schoolteachers too must make some of the sacrifices needed to get the Senegalese economy back on its feet.

The Etats Généraux de l'Enseignement was an enormous success for the Diouf regime. The government's conciliatory stance and willingness to repudiate some of Senghor's most cherished educational policies disarmed SUDES and the opposition and was widely acclaimed by the general public. The conference reduced tensions in the country and created the atmosphere for a new dialogue between the government and the opposition. A few months later, the government lifted the sanctions it had previously taken against the SUDES schoolteachers.

One of the major problems Diouf had to face upon taking power was how to deal with the political opposition. During the last days of the Senghor era, the opposition had challenged Diouf's right to assume the presidency without going before the people in a national election and stepped up its attacks against the regime for its undemocratic behavior in not granting the "illegal" opposition parties the formal recognition needed to compete openly with Senegal's legal parties. The deteriorating economic situation, growing urban discontent, and the prospects of Senghor's departure spurred the opposition's militancy. At the same time, elements within the right wing of the PS were calling for a crackdown on the opposition and hinting that the country might be better off with a one-party system, with the PS as the sole party. At a Club Nation et Développement conference held in Dakar in December 1980, the main speaker warned that Senegal's fragile democracy was in grave danger of being transformed into a dictatorship and recommended that the opposition tone down its threats in order to not give right-wing elements an excuse to seize power.

Instead of cracking down on the opposition, Diouf opted to liberalize the regime by moving to bring the illegal opposition into the system. In late March 1981, he announced that he would ask the National Assembly to authorize the recognition of all political parties. In April, the National Assembly voted to eliminate the constitutional provision limiting the number of legal political parties to four.[14] And in June the government formally recognized Cheikh Anta Diop's RND, which had been fighting for legal status since 1976, and several smaller parties on Senegal's fragmented left. By 1982, the number of legal opposition parties had jumped to eleven.

The liberalization measures took some of the steam out of the opposition and weakened the position of Abdoulaye Wade, leader of the PDS. Wade had called upon the army to intervene to ensure free and fair elections to determine who would succeed Senghor. This appeal to the army fell flat[15] and antagonized many Senegalese who did not wish to see a precedent set for justifying military intervention. Wade also failed in his attempts to unify Senegal's political opposition under his banner. Opposition elements on the left did not see Wade as a viable alternative to Senghor; indeed, many saw his candidacy as a clever ploy devised by Senghor to split the opposition. As it became more evident that Diouf was gaining popularity in the country, Wade began to have problems within his own party. Several PDS deputies quit to rally to the PS. Wade and his party lost further ground when he fled to France during the latter part of 1981 in the face of government charges that members of his party had received paramilitary training in Libya. Wade's return to Senegal at the beginning of 1982 was accompanied by more resignations from his party and the rallying of several PDS deputies to the PS. By the middle of 1982, the number of PDS deputies in the National Assembly had fallen to ten, well below the fifteen needed to constitute a parliamentary group with the right to be represented on all committees.

With the formerly illegal political parties permitted to operate freely, the political opposition will probably remain fragmented. It is highly unlikely that strong personalities and long-time rivals like Cheikh Anta Diop and Mamadou Dia will join forces when they can lead their own legal political parties and compete for power. With the opposition back in the electoral game and split into many contending groups and factions, Diouf was placed in a good position to play off one group against the other to preserve the position of the PS as Senegal's majority party after the national elections scheduled for early 1983.

Although Abdou Diouf succeeded remarkably well in asserting his authority, defusing tensions, and containing the political opposition during his first few months in office, he still had to solve the problem of how to rejuvenate his party while holding the various factions together. Diouf and his closest political allies were members of the circle of technocrats and intellectuals that Senghor brought into the government during the late 1960s and 1970s. With Senghor's backing, they had displaced most of the old guard as regional and local leaders. Yet, as technocrats spending most of their time running the state bureaucracy, they had few close ties with the party faithful at the grassroots levels. The lack of contact with the less educated and more traditionalist rank and file members of the party was largely due to the fact that Diouf and the relatively young, well-educated, cosmopolitan group around him defined themselves as members of a national intellectual elite rather than the representatives of local, regional, and ethnic constituencies.

With Senghor gone and opposition parties now free to compete for the votes of Senegal's rural population, Diouf and his allies must make a greater effort to reach out and win the support of local, regional, ethnic, and religious constituencies if they are to retain power. This has meant more frequent trips to the interior on the part of government ministers and a greater effort to display more "traditional" lifestyles and modes of dealing with the party's clientele. Thus, since assuming office, Prime Minister Habib Thiam, once the epitome of the aloof, urbane Dakar sophisticate, dons the *grand boubou* of the pious Muslim more frequently and mingles warmly with the masses when appearing in public.

Diouf and his circle of allies have also tried to make the party more attractive to urban and rural youth. Whereas the old guard tended to give young party members few responsibilities when it dominated party politics during the first decade of independence, Diouf has made a concerted effort to mobilize PS youth groups throughout the country and to give them a greater voice in party affairs. He has also stepped up the organizing of women's groups, especially in the countryside. Diouf's educational reforms and promises to provide more jobs for unemployed secondary school and university graduates were, in part, designed to win over the large segment of Senegal's educated youth who had turned their backs on the Senghor regime and given their sympathies to the opposition.

Perhaps most crucial to Diouf's political survival and that of the PS as Senegal's ruling party will be his ability to retain the backing of the powerful Muslim brotherhoods, which had been one of the main pillars of the Senghor regime. Since taking office, Diouf, who is a Tijani, has courted the Mourides, whose numbers and influence have grown considerably under the dynamic leadership of Abdoul Lahat M'Backé.[16] By 1982 Diouf had won the esteem of the leaders of Senegal's most prominent brotherhoods. The brotherhoods themselves seemed to be on better terms with each other than at any time since independence and were apparently uniting behind Diouf.

Diouf is counting upon the collaboration of the marabouts to defuse peasant discontent, particularly in the peanut basin, and to ensure the participation of the rural masses in the government's rural development programs. Diouf and the PS also need the support of the marabouts and the countryside as a counterweight to Dakar, where the party has always been relatively weaker and where popular discontent is likely to grow because of downward pressures on urban living standards caused by the application of the government's austerity programs. Hence, it was not difficult to understand why the government canceled peasant debts, sharply raised producers' prices for peanuts and other agricultural commodities, and stepped up the number of community development projects after the disastrous 1980-1981 agricultural season.

Diouf is counting upon retaining the loyalty of the military. Although Senghor was not above using the armed forces to crush strikes and student demonstrations, he did manage to keep the military out of politics and develop its sense of professionalism and commitment to civilian authority. Thus far, the military has turned a deaf ear to appeals by the radical opposition to rally to its cause. It is highly unlikely that the military will intervene politically unless there is a major breakdown in order. Even then, the military would be more likely to sustain the Diouf regime rather than bring it down.

Diouf's success in asserting his authority and initiating popular political and educational reforms during his first year in office did much to stabilize the country and avert the specter of a violent confrontation between the regime and its opponents that was looming on the horizon just before Senghor departed. In mid-1982 Diouf seemed to be firmly in control of the country and he and his party likely winners in the 1983 national elections. Notwithstanding Diouf's popularity, Senegal still rested on shaky political ground; the economic crisis, if left unresolved, could once again touch off widespread popular unrest.

PROSPECTS FOR THE FUTURE: TOWARD THE YEAR 2000

Senegal entered the 1980s with gloomy prospects for reaching the ambitious goals set by Senghor for the year 2000. During the 1980s, the Senegalese economy will be heavily mortgaged to the IMF and other foreign creditors. The export economy based on the peanut monoculture Senegal inherited from the colonial era is clearly no longer capable of sustaining the country. And a new postcolonial economy based on agricultural modernization and a diversified economy has not yet managed to replace it. In its march toward the twenty-first century Senegal will be going through a difficult period of economic readjustment and transformation.

Despite Senegal's current economic difficulties, there is a strong current of anticipation about the future flowing through the country. Economic crisis has intensified the desire for change and efforts to break out of the confines of the old colonial economy. Many young cadres are eager to renovate Senegalese agricultural research and work more closely with the peasantry. For their part, the rural people have become less docile and less willing to accept the dictates of the state without having their views taken into consideration. They have already demonstrated their capacity to modernize agricultural techniques and improve productivity when they are given economic incentives and rainfall is sufficient. Rural reforms are now under way to decentralize decision making and reduce the weight of the state bureaucracy.

By mid-1982, major dam projects were under way. As a result, by the end of the century the locus of Senegal's rural economy will move from the peanut basin to the regions that were neglected during the colonial period and the early years of independence. This shift will occur whether the massive dam projects prove to be a financial and ecological disaster or a marvelous success. The die is cast.

As Senegal moves toward the year 2000, the relative importance of the peanut oil and import-substitution industries, which sparked much

of Senegal's industrial development during the first two decades of independence, will decline. Export-oriented industries and the transformation of Senegal's phosphate and iron ore resources will become the basis
for a new wave of economic growth that will depend largely upon
Senegal's ability to attract foreign capital, develop cheaper sources of
energy, and gain greater access to European and African markets.
Despite efforts to decentralize industrial development, Dakar and the
Cap Vert peninsula will continue as the main hub of economic activity.
The economic gap between Maritime and Sahelian Senegal will probably
continue to widen.

    Population growth is emerging as an important issue in Senegal. In
1980, Senegal's population was estimated to be 5.9 million and growing
at an annual rate of more than 2.6 percent.[17] By the year 2000, Senegal's
population will soar to nearly 10 million. By then 40 percent of the people will be living in urban areas and Greater Dakar will have a population of more than 3 million. It remains to be seen whether Senegal will be
able to generate sufficient economic growth to provide adequate food,
housing, health care, schooling, and jobs to meet the needs of the country's booming population.

    Even if the vast development projects being pursued in the early
1980s by the Senegalese government prove to be successful, it is still not
clear whether most Senegalese will benefit from the sweeping changes
they will bring. For example, the dam and irrigation projects designed to
open up thousands of hectares of land for cultivation in the Casamance
and the Senegal River valley could conceivably touch off an agricultural
revolution by providing landless peasants with land and small-scale
family farmers with higher standards of living and greater control of
their economic destinies. On the other hand, they could also reinforce
the hold of the state bureaucracy over the peasantry, foster land grabs by
local notables and unscrupulous government officials, and perpetuate
Senegal's growing dependency upon international capital.[18] Moreover, it
is possible for Senegal to develop its mining resources and achieve high
industrial growth rates without reducing unemployment or improving
the wages and living standards of the urban masses. It is more likely that
most of the benefits of industrial development will be captured by
foreign and Senegalese capitalists and managers rather than be spread
throughout the economy, with Senegalese workers sharing in the profits
and the Senegalese elite sharing some of the sacrifices.

    Senegalese society is in flux and moving rapidly to assert its own
national identity. By the year 2000 this will bear little resemblance to the
colonial Senegal that the new nation began to leave behind in 1960. By
the year 2000, 80 percent of Senegal's population will have been born

after independence, and only a tiny fraction of the national leadership will have experienced growing up under colonial rule.

The clash between Western and Islamic cultures is likely to intensify. During the colonial period, Islam was a conservative and stabilizing force in Senegalese society, content to make its peace with colonial society in exchange for cultural autonomy. Today, Islam is once again on the move in Senegal, challenging the alleged superiority of the Western values held by the secularized Senegalese elite now in power. Islam could very well become a new rallying point for Senegalese political and cultural nationalism, as it was during the nineteenth century. Indeed, there are some signs that Diouf and the new generation of Senegalese assuming power in the early 1980s are "re-Islamizing" their value systems and lifestyles.

Despite Islam's rising status, it is highly unlikely that Senegal will be transformed into a radical Islamic republic led by a Khomeini-like religious leader or a Kaddafi. The leaders of Senegal's Muslim brotherhoods are likely to work out a modus vivendi among themselves and between themselves and the government rather than agitate for radical religious reforms. At the same time, the westernized elite is no longer as willing to accept French cultural hegemony or to blindly emulate Western lifestyles. The growing interest in promoting adult literacy in the national languages and the use of the national languages in the schools are clear signs of movement toward greater cultural nationalism. Moreover, the demand of many Senegalese intellectuals to have Wolof replace French as the national language and the official working language of the state bureaucracy reflects a strong desire to assert a distinctly Senegalese national identity and break away from the colonial past.

In international relations, Senegal under Diouf is likely to pursue an activist foreign policy along the same lines as his predecessor.[19] With Senghor gone and given the resurgence of Islam throughout the Third World, Senegal will develop its Islamic identity and move closer to the Muslim world without loosening its ties to the rest of Black Africa. Senegal will probably continue to maintain its special relationship with France. The election of François Mitterrand and the coming to power of of the French Socialists[20] in 1981 suggest that France will adopt a less paternalistic stance in dealing with Senegal and other Third World countries. Its pro–Third World foreign policy and willingness to raise the volume of economic aid is likely to increase France's popularity in Senegal.

Senegal's future stability and the survival of one of Black Africa's most promising experiments in political democracy will depend to a large extent upon the Diouf regime's ability to resolve Senegal's deep economic crisis. Senegal's excellent relations with the Arab oil-producing countries, the coming to power of a Socialist government in France, and the Reagan administration's growing interest in Senegal as a strategic and staunchly anticommunist African nation provided Senegal with additional aid and resources during the early 1980s. However, more aid alone will not be sufficient; the Diouf regime also needs to retain the support of the people and demonstrate that there is some hope for a better future, despite Senegal's economic difficulties.

Although the road toward the year 2000 promises to be rough and rocky, it is not beyond the capacity of the Senegalese to work out their own synthesis of traditional African, Islamic, and Western values and to find solutions to the difficult political and economic dilemma that they must face without abandoning political democracy and the hopes for a new and more equitable postcolonial economic order.

NOTES

1. Senghor's report was published as *Le plan du décollage économique ou la participation responsable comme moteur du développement* [The economic take-off plan or responsible participation as the motor for development] (Dakar: Grande Imprimerie Africaine, n.d.).

2. See the analysis of Senegal's agricultural situation at the end of the 1980-1981 season in *Marchés Tropicaux*, May 15, 1981, pp. 1356-1357.

3. Ibid., p. 1357.

4. For example, see "La relance de la dépendance" [The revival of dependence], *Andë Sopi*, No. 37 (June 1980):5-6.

5. For a detailed analysis of the *grands projets*, see "L'heure des grands projets" [The hour of big projects], *Jeune Afrique*, No. 689 (March 23, 1974):30-33.

6. *Marchés Tropicaux*, April 10, 1981, p. 999.

7. *Bulletin de l'Afrique Noire*, No. 1095 (June 3, 1981):20953.

8. See the special April 17, 1981, issue of *Marchés Tropicaux* on the OMVS for full details about the Diama and Manantali dam projects.

9. *Marchés Tropicaux*, April 17, 1981, p. 1124.

10. On this point, see *Afrique Nouvelle*, January 7-11, 1981, pp. 15-17.

11. See, for example, "Abdou Diouf va jouer l'ouverture" [Abdou Diouf to make political overtures], *Jeune Afrique*, No. 1045 (January 14, 1981):15-19.

12. For an account of Diouf's triumphant trip and general success during his first months in office, see "Les 100 jours ou le safara d'Abdou" [Abdou's first 100 days], *Africa*, No. 130 (April 1981):31-32.

13. For a detailed analysis of this historic conference, see *Afrique Nouvelle*, February 11-17, 1981, pp. 14-18 and 26.

14. The constitutional revision permitted the four existing parties to drop the labels previously attributed to them by law if they wished. It also forbade the

creation of any political party based on race, ethnicity, sex, language, religion, or regional affiliation. *Marchés Tropicaux*, May 1, 1981, p. 1243.

15. *Afrique Nouvelle*, No. 1045 (January 14, 1981):19.

16. To demonstrate his even-handedness, Diouf, who has close ties to the Sy dynasty in Tivaoune, named Médoune Fall, a Mouride, to be minister of the interior and Moustapha Niasse, who is related to the Niasse dynasty of Kaolack, to be the minister of foreign affairs.

17. *Marchés Tropicaux*, April 17, 1981, p. 1124.

18. For example, see Jean Copans, "From Senegambia to Senegal: The Evolution of Peasantries," in Martin A. Klein, ed., *Peasants in Africa: Historical and Contemporary Perspectives* (Beverly Hills, Calif.: Sage Publications, 1980), pp. 77–103; and Adrian Adams, "The Senegal River Valley: What Kind of Change?" *Review of African Political Economy*, No. 10 (September-December 1977):33–59.

19. Since resigning, Senghor himself has continued to play an active role on the international scene, serving as Senegal's elder statesman in promoting a pro-Western inter-African socialist movement and his long-cherished dream of creating a francophone commonwealth.

20. Senegal's special relationship with France will doubtless be helped by the fact that the French Socialists and the PS are both members of the Socialist International.

Selected Bibliography

GENERAL WORKS

Biarnès, Pierre. *L'Afrique aux africains: 20 ans d'indépendance en Afrique Noire Francophone* [Africa for the Africans: Twenty years of independence in francophone Black Africa]. Paris: Armand Colin, 1980.

Colvin, Lucie Gallistel. *Historical Dictionary of Senegal*. Metuchen, N.J.: Scarecrow Press, 1981.

Hargreaves, John D. *West Africa: The Former French States*. Englewood Cliffs, N.J.: Prentice-Hall, 1967.

Lavroff, Dmitri-Georges. *La République du Sénégal* [The republic of Senegal]. Paris: R. Pichon & R. Durand-Auzias, 1966.

Lusignan, Guy de. *French-Speaking Africa Since Independence*. New York: Frederick A. Praeger, 1969.

Nelson, Harold D., et al. *U.S. Army Handbook for Senegal*. 2nd ed. Washington, D.C.: Government Printing Office, 1974.

Senegal, Republic of. *Atlas national du Sénégal* [National atlas of Senegal]. Paris: Institut de Géographie National, 1977.

HISTORY

Barry, Boubacar. *Le royaume du Waalo: Le Sénégal avant la conquête* [The kingdom of Waalo: Senegal before the conquest]. Paris: François Maspero, 1972.

Cohen, William B. *Rulers of Empire: The French Colonial Service in Africa*. Stanford, Calif.: Stanford University Press, 1971.

Crowder, Michael. *Senegal: A Study of French Assimilation Policy*. London: Oxford University Press, 1962.

Curtin, Philip. *Economic Change in Precolonial Africa: Senegambia in the Era of the Slave Trade*. Madison: University of Wisconsin Press, 1975.

Delavignette, Robert. *Freedom and Authority in French West Africa*. London: Oxford University Press, 1950.

Diagne, Pathé. *Pouvoir politique traditionelle en Afrique Occidentale* [Traditional political power in West Africa]. Paris: Présence Africaine, 1967.

Diop, Cheikh Anta. *L'Afrique noire pré-Coloniale* [Precolonial Black Africa]. Paris: Présence Africaine, 1960.

Gellar, Sheldon. *Structural Changes and Colonial Dependency: Senegal 1885–1945.* Beverly Hills, Calif.: Sage Publications, 1976.

Johnson, G. Wesley, Jr. *The Emergence of Black Politics in Senegal: The Struggle for Power in the Four Communes, 1900–1920.* Stanford, Calif.: Stanford University Press, 1971.

Klein, Martin A. *Islam and Imperialism in Senegal: Sine-Saloum, 1847–1914.* Stanford, Calif.: Stanford University Press, 1968.

———— . "Social and Economic Factors in the Muslim Revolution in Senegambia." *Journal of African History* 13, 3 (1972):419–441.

Robinson, David W. *Clerics and Chiefs: The History of Abdul Bokar Kane and the Futa Toro.* New York: Oxford University Press, 1976.

Suret-Canale, Jean. *Afrique noire occidentale et centrale: L'ère coloniale, 1900–1945* [West and Central Africa: The colonial era, 1900–1945]. Paris: Editions Sociales, 1964.

Trimingham, J. Spencer. *A History of Islam in West Africa.* London: Oxford University Press, 1962.

POLITICS AND GOVERNMENT

Barker, Jonathan S. "The Paradox of Development: Reflections on a Study of Local-Central Political Relations in Senegal." In *The State of the Nations,* pp. 47–63. Edited by Michael F. Lofchie. Berkeley: University of California Press, 1971.

———— . "Political Factionalism in Senegal." *Canadian Journal of African Studies* 7, 2 (1973):287–303.

Club Nation et Développement. *Club Nation et Développement* [Club for development and the nation]. Paris: Présence Africaine, 1972.

Cottingham, Clement. "Political Consolidation and Centre-Local Relations in Senegal." *Canadian Journal of African Studies* 4, 1 (Winter 1970):101–120.

Fall, Ibrahima. *Sous-développement et démocratie multipartisane, L'experience sénégalaise* [Underdevelopment and multiparty democracy: The Senegalese experience]. Dakar: Nouvelles Editions Africaines, 1977.

Foltz, William J. *From French West Africa to the Mali Federation.* New Haven, Conn.: Yale University Press, 1965.

———— . "Senegal." In *Political Parties and National Integration in Tropical Africa,* pp. 16–64. Edited by James S. Coleman and Carl G. Rosberg, Jr. Berkeley: University of California Press, 1964.

———— . "Social Structure and Political Behavior of Senegalese Elites." *Behavior Science Notes* 4, 2 (1969):145–163.

Gautron, Jean-Claude, and Rougevin-Baville, Michel. *Droit public du Sénégal* [Senegalese public law]. Paris: Editions A. Pedone, 1970.

Gellar, Sheldon. "The Politics of Development in Senegal." Ph.D. dissertation, Columbia University, 1967.

———— . "State-Building and Nation-Building in West Africa." In *Building States and Nations: Models, Analyses, and Data Across Three Worlds,* Vol. 2, pp. 384–426. Edited by S. N. Eisenstadt and Stein Rokkan. Beverly Hills, Calif.: Sage Publications, 1973.

Markovitz, Irving L. *Léopold Sédar Senghor and the Politics of Negritude.* New York: Atheneum, 1969.

N'Diaye, Jean-Pierre. *Enquête sur les étudiants noirs en France* [A survey of Black African students in France]. Paris: Editions Réalités Africaines, 1962.

_____. *La jeunesse africaine face à l'imperialism* [African youth confronting imperialism]. Paris: François Maspero, 1971.

O'Brien, Donal B. Cruise. *Saints and Politicians: Essays in the Organization of a Senegalese Peasant Society.* London: Cambridge University Press, 1975.

_____. "Senegal." In *West African States: Failure and Promise,* pp. 173–188. Edited by John Dunn. Cambridge: Cambridge University Press, 1978.

O'Brien, Rita Cruise (ed.). *The Political Economy of Underdevelopment: Dependence in Senegal.* Beverly Hills, Calif.: Sage Publications, 1979.

Robinson, Kenneth. "Senegal." In *Five Elections in Africa,* pp. 281–390. Edited by W.J.K. Mackenzie and Kenneth Robinson. London: Oxford University Press, 1960.

Schachter-Morgenthau, Ruth. *Political Parties in French-Speaking West Africa.* London: Oxford University Press, 1964.

Schumacher, Edward J. *Politics, Bureaucracy, and Rural Development in Senegal.* Berkeley: University of California Press, 1975.

Zuccarelli, François. *Un parti politique africain: L'Union Progressiste Sénégalaise* [An African political party: The Senegalese Progressive Union]. Paris: R. Pichon & R. Durand-Auzias, 1970.

THE ECONOMY

Adams, Adrian. "The Senegal River Valley: What Kind of Change?" *Review of African Political Economy,* No. 10 (September-December 1977):33–59.

Amin, Samir. *L'Afrique de L'Ouest bloquée* [The blocking of West African development]. Paris: Editions de Minuit, 1971.

_____. *Le monde des affaires sénégalais* [The Senegalese business world]. Paris: Editions de Minuit, 1969.

Diarrasouba, Valy-Charles. *L'évolution des structures agricoles du Sénégal* [The evolution of Senegalese agricultural structures]. Paris: Editions Cujas, 1968.

Gellar, Sheldon, Charlick, Robert B., and Jones, Yvonne. *Animation Rurale and Rural Development: The Experience of Senegal.* Ithaca, N.Y.: Cornell University Rural Development Committee, 1980.

Hopkins, A. G. *An Economic History of West Africa.* New York: Columbia University Press, 1973.

International Monetary Fund. *Surveys of African Economies: Dahomey, Ivory Coast, Mauritania, Niger, Senegal, Togo, Vol. 3.* Washington, D.C.: International Monetary Fund, 1970.

I.R.F.E.D. *Le Sénégal en marche: Le plan de développement* [Senegal on the move: The development plan]. Paris: Editions Création de Presse, 1961.

O'Brien, Rita Cruise. "Foreign Ascendance in the Economy and State: The French and Lebanese." In *The Political Economy of Underdevelopment: Dependence in Senegal,* pp. 100–125. Edited by Rita Cruise O'Brien. Beverly Hills, Calif.: Sage Publications, 1979.

_____ . "Lebanese Entrepreneurs in Senegal: Economic Integration and the Politics of Protection." *Cahiers d'Etudes Africaines* 15, 57 (1975):95–115.

Pfefferman, Guy. *Industrial Labor in the Republic of Senegal*. New York: Frederick A. Praeger, 1968.

Senegal, Republic of. *Cinquième Plan Quadriennal de Développement Economique et Social (1ᵉʳ juillet 1977–30 juin 1981)* [Fifth four-year economic and social development plan (1 July 1977–30 June 1981)]. Dakar: Nouvelles Editions Africaines, 1977.

_____ . *Le Sénégal en chiffres, éditions 1978* [Senegal in figures, 1978 edition]. Dakar: Société Africaine d'Editions, 1979.

Senghor, Léopold Sédar. *On African Socialism*. New York: Frederick A. Praeger, 1964.

Thomas, Louis-Vincent (ed.). *Prospective du développement en Afrique noire, Un scenario: Le Sénégal* [Development prospective in Black Africa, a scenario: The Senegal case]. Paris: Presses Universitaires de France, 1978.

Vanhaeverbeke, André. *Rémuneration du travail et commerce extérieur: Essor d'une économie exportatrice et termes de l'échange des producteurs d'arachides au Sénégal* [Remuneration of labor and foreign trade: Progress of an Export Economy and the terms of trade of peanut producers in Senegal]. Louvain: Centre de Recherches des Pays en Développement, 1970.

World Bank. *Senegal: Tradition, Diversification, and Economic Development*. Washington, D.C.: World Bank, 1974.

SENEGAL AND THE WORLD

Biarnès, Pierre. "La diplomatie sénégalaise" [Senegalese diplomacy]. *Revue Française d'Etudes Politiques Africaines*, No. 149 (1978):62–78.

Bourgi, Albert. *La politique française de coopération en Afrique: Le cas du Sénégal* [French aid policy in Africa: The Senegal case]. Paris: R. Pichon & R. Durand-Auzias, 1979.

Club du Sahel/CILSS. *Official Development Assistance to CILSS Member Countries from 1975–1979*, Vol. I. Paris: Club du Sahel, 1980.

Colvin, Lucie Gallistel. "International Relations in Precolonial Senegal." *Présence Africaine*, No. 93 (1975):215–230.

Dia, Mamadou. *The African Nations and World Solidarity*. New York: Frederick A. Praeger, 1961.

Mortimer, Edward. *France and the Africans, 1944–1960: A Political History*. New York: Walker and Company, 1969.

Senghor, Léopold Sédar. *La poésie de l'action, conversations avec Mohamed Aziza* [The poetry of action: Conversations with Mohamed Aziza]. Paris: Editions Stock, 1980.

Skurnik, W.A.E. *The Foreign Policy of Senegal*. Evanston, Ill.: Northwestern University Press, 1972.

Thiam, Doudou. *The Foreign Policy of African States*. New York: Frederick A. Praeger, 1965.

Tunteng, P-Kiven. "External Influences and Subimperialism in Francophone West Africa." In *The Political Economy of Contemporary Africa*, pp. 212–231. Edited by Peter C. W. Gutkind and Immanuel Wallerstein. Beverly Hills,

Calif.: Sage Publications, 1976.

White, Dorothy S. *Black Africa and De Gaulle: From the French Empire to Independence*. University Park: Pennsylvania State University Press, 1979.

SOCIAL STRUCTURES

Adams, Adrian. *Le long voyage des gens du fleuve Sénégal* [The long journey of the Senegal River people]. Paris: François Maspero, 1977.

Behrman, Lucy C. *Muslim Brotherhoods and Politics in Senegal*. Cambridge, Mass.: Harvard University Press, 1970.

Boutillier, J. L., et al. *La moyenne vallée du Sénégal* [The middle valley of the Senegal River]. Paris: Presses Universitaires de France, 1962.

Colvin, Lucie Gallistel (ed.). *The Uprooted of the Western Sahel: Migrants' Quest for Cash in the Senegambia*. New York: Praeger Publishers, 1981.

Copans, Jean. "From Senegambia to Senegal: The Evolution of Peasantries." In *Peasants in Africa: Historical and Contemporary Perspectives*, pp. 76–103. Edited by Martin A. Klein. Beverly Hills, Calif.: Sage Publications, 1980.

Diop, Majhemout. *Histoire des classes sociales dans L'Afrique de L'Ouest: Le Sénégal* [History of social classes in West Africa: Senegal]. Paris: François Maspero, 1972.

Fougeyrollas, Pierre. *Où va le Sénégal? Une analyse spectrale d'une nation africaine* [Where is Senegal going? A spectrum analysis of an African nation]. Paris: Editions Anthropos, 1970.

Kane, Francine. "Femmes Proletaires du Senegal, a la ville et aux champs" [Proletarian women of Senegal in the city and the countryside]. *Cahiers d'Etudes Africaines* 17, 65 (1976):77–94.

O'Brien, Donal B. Cruise. *The Mourides of Senegal: The Political and Economic Organization of an Islamic Brotherhood*. London: Oxford University Press, 1971.

O'Brien, Rita Cruise. *White Society in Black Africa: The French of Senegal*. Evanston, Ill.: Northwestern University Press, 1972.

Pélissier, Paul. *Les paysans du Sénégal: Les civilisations agraires du Cayor à la Casamance* [Peasants of Senegal: Agrarian civilizations from Cayor to the Casamance]. Saint-Yrieix: Imprimerie Fabrègue, 1966.

Sankalé, Marc (ed.). *Dakar en Devenir* [Dakar in evolution]. Paris: Présence Africaine, 1968.

Silla, Ousemane. "Persistance des castes dans la société Wolof contemporaine" [The persistence of caste in contemporary Wolof society]. *Bulletin de L'I.F.A.N.* 28 (Series B), 3–4 (1966):731–770.

Sy, Cheikh Tidiane. *La confrérie sénégalaise des Mourides* [The Senegalese Mouride brotherhood]. Paris: Présence Africaine, 1969.

Winder, R. Bayly. "The Lebanese in West Africa." *Comparative Studies in Society and History* 4, 3 (April 1962):296–333.

CULTURE

Ba, Mariama. *Une si longue lettre* [A very long letter]. Dakar: Nouvelles Editions Africaines, 1980.

Blondé, Jacques, Dumont, Pierre, and Gontier, Dominique. *Lexique du français du Sénégal* [Lexicon of Senegalese French]. Dakar: Nouvelles Editions Africaines, 1979.

Dia, Mamadou. *Islam, sociétés africaines, et cultures industrielles* [Islam, African societies, and industrial cultures]. Dakar: Nouvelles Editions Africaines, 1975.

Diop, Birago. *Les contes d'Amadou-Koumba* [Tales of Amadou-Koumba]. Paris: Présence Africaine, 1961.

Diop, Cheikh Anta. *Nations nègres et culture* [Black nations and culture]. Paris: Présence Africaine, 1955.

Diop, Ousemane Socé. *Karim*. Paris: Nouvelles Editions Latines, 1948.

Fall, Aminata Sow. *La Grève des Battù* [The strike of the beggars]. Dakar: Nouvelles Editions Africaines, 1980.

Fougeyrollas, Pierre. *Modernisation des hommes, L'exemple du Sénégal* [The modernization of man, the example of Senegal]. Paris: Flammarion, 1967.

Hymans, Jacques Louis. *Léopold Sédar Senghor: An Intellectual Biography*. Edinburgh: Edinburgh University Press, 1971.

Kane, Cheikh Hamidou. *Ambiguous Adventure*. New York: Collier Books, 1969.

Sembène, Ousemane. *God's Bits of Wood*. Garden City, N.Y.: Anchor Books, 1970.

Senghor, Léopold Sédar. *Ethiopiques*. Paris: Editions du Seuil, 1956.

————— . *Nocturnes*. Paris: Editions du Seuil, 1961.

Sylla, Assane. *La philosophie morale des Wolof* [The moral philosophy of the Wolof]. Dakar: Sankoré, 1978.

Abbreviations

BDS	Bloc Démocratique Sénégalais
BMS	Bloc des Masses Sénégalais
BPS	Bloc Populaire Sénégalais
BSD	Banque Sénégalaise de Développement
CEAO	West African Economic Community
CLAD	Centre de Linguistique Appliquée de Dakar
CNTS	Confederation Nationale des Travailleurs Sénégalais
COFEGES	Conseil Federal des Groupements Economiques du Sénégal
ECOWAS	Economic Community of West African States
EDF	European Fund
EEC	European Economic Community
FIDES	Economic and Social Development Investment Fund
FNS	Front National Sénégalais
GES	Groupements Economiques du Sénégal
ICS	Industries Chimiques du Sénégal
IMF	International Monetary Fund
IOM	Independants d'Outre-Mer
MIFERSO	Mines de Fer du Sénégal Oriental
MRP	Mouvement Républicain Populaire
MRS	Mouvement Républicain Sénégalais
NIEO	New International Economic Order

OAU	Organization of African Unity
OCA	Office de Commercialisation Agricole
OCAM	Organisation Commune Africaine et Malgache
OMVG	Organisation de Mise en Valeur du Fleuve Gambie
OMVS	Organisation de Mise en Valeur du Fleuve Sénégal
ONCAD	Office National de Coopération d'Assistance au Développement
OPEC	Organization of Petroleum Exporting Countries
PAI	Parti Africain de l'Indépendance
PAIGC	African Independence Party of Guinea and Cap Vert
PDS	Parti Démocratique Sénégalais
PLO	Palestine Liberation Organization
PRA–Sénégal	Parti du Rassemblement Africain – Sénégal
PS	Parti Socialiste
PSS	Parti Socialiste Sénégalais
RDA	Rassemblement Démocratique Africain
RDAs	Regional Development Agencies
RND	Rassemblement National Démocratique
SFIO	French Socialist party
SMIG	Salaire Minimum Interprofessionnelle Guaranti
SNES	Syndicat National des Enseignants du Sénégal
SONEPI	Société Nationale d'Etudes et de Promotion Industrielle
SONOCOS	Société Nationale de Commercialisation des Oléaginaux du Sénégal
SOPRIZI	Société d'aménagement et de Promotion de la zone franche industrielle de Dakar
SUDES	Syndicat Unique et Démocrate des Enseignants du Sénégal
UGTAN	Union Générale des Travailleurs Sénégalais
UNCTAD	United Nations Conference on Trade and Development

UNESCO	United Nations Educational, Scientific and Cultural Organization
UNIGES	Union des Groupements Economiques du Sénégal
UNTS	Union National des Travailleurs Sénégalais
UPS	Union Progressiste Sénégalais
USB	Union Sénégalaise de Banque
UTLS	Union des Travailleurs Libres du Sénégal

Index

Abu Dhabi, 79
Administrative Reform (1972), 31, 41–42
Afghanistan, 82
Africa, 71–78, 82
African Assembly Party of Senegal. *See* Parti du Rassemblement Africain-Sénégal
African Democratic Assembly. *See* Rassemblement Démocratique Africain
African Independence Party. *See* Parti Africain de l'Indépendance
African Independence Party of Guinea and Cap Vert (PAIGC), 73, 74
Africanization, 39, 53–55, 69
African Socialism, 30–31, 41, 57–59, 84, 93
Agriculture, 46, 52
  diversification of, 48–50
  future of, 121, 122
  modernization of, 121
  productivity, 112
  railroads and, 13–14, 15
  young people and, 104
  See also Peanuts
Al Azar University, 91
Algeria, 77–78
Algiers Conference, 81
Almoravid movement, 2
al-Tijani, Ahmad, 6–7
Angola, 77–78, 82, 83
Animation Feminine, 103
Animation Rurale. *See* Rural Animation program
Applied Linguistics Center of Dakar. *See* Centre de Linguistique Appliquée de Dakar
Arab Bank for Economic Development in Africa, 79
Arab-Israeli conflict, 79
Arabization, 73

Arab League, 73
Arab world. *See* Islamic world
Arafat, Yassir, 67
Argentina, 81
Army, 38, 120
Artisan castes, 4
Assimilationism, 9–10, 11, 12, 13

Ba, Boubacar, 28–29
Ba, Mariama, 102
Bamba, Amadou, 8, 12, 13, 88, 89, 91, 92
Bangladesh, 81
Banque Nationale du Développement Sénégalais (BNDS), 37, 66(n8)
Banque Sénégalaise de Développement (BSD), 53, 66(n8)
Baol, 4
Basic Research Institute of Black Africa. *See* Institut Fondamental d'Afrique Noire
BDS. *See* Bloc Démocratique Sénégalaise
Benin, 75
Berlin Congress, 9
Bloc Démocratique Sénégalaise (BDS), 18, 19
Bloc des Masses Sénégalaises (BMS), 25
Bloc of the Senegalese Masses. *See* Bloc des Masses Sénégalaises
Bloc Populaire Sénégalaise (BPS), 19–20
BMS. *See* Bloc des Masses Sénégalaises
BNDS. *See* Banque Nationale du Développement Sénégalais
Bourguiba, Habib, 77
BPS. *See* Bloc Populaire Sénégalaise
Brazil, 81
Brazzaville Conference (1944), 17
BSD. *See* Banque Sénégalaise de Développement
BUD-Sénégal, 56, 103
Business. *See* Private sector

137